HistoricBoise

An Introduction to the Architecture of Boise, Idaho, 1863-1938

Arthur A. Hart

Historic Idaho, Inc.

Historic Idaho, Inc.
Boise, Idaho
1993

This is the fourth printing of a book originally published in 1979 as part of the Boise City Historic Preservation Plan. Charles F. Hummel, F.A.I.A. was project coordinator.

Library of Congress Catalog Card No. 79-91082

ISBN 0-9631258-2-6

Historic Idaho, Inc., an Idaho non-profit organization, is dedicated to the publication of works on Idaho history and culture. Proceeds from sales are used to publish additional works on Idaho.

TABLE OF CONTENTS

THE CITY OF BOISE, IDAHO FOUNDED 1863

2

2.
The Boise City Seal is evidently taken from a mural in the Council Chambers of the 1893 City Hall. The decorations were painted by Max Kohn. The earliest city document showing the seal is dated May 1894. The origin of the motto "Peril – Energy – Success" is unknown. The central emblem with the figures of an army officer and miner recall the establishment of the city as a fort and outfitting camp for the Boise Basin. The symbols in the central emblem include a mountain scene and river, a medical symbol, a shock of wheat and a horn of plenty with gold coins spilling from it. The beaver above the emblem recalls the term "Beaver Territory" – a name given to Idaho by the early trappers of the Hudson's Bay Company.

FOREWORD
to the Fourth Printing

Historic Boise is a brief introduction to the architectural legacy of Idaho's capital city from its founding in 1863 to the eve of World War II. It is architectural history at its best because it shows that buildings have dimensions which go beyond mere descriptions of size or style. Good buildings have a dimension in time that persists beyond the life of the builder or original owner. They also have economic, social and artistic dimensions that frequently become more interesting and valuable with age. These qualities, when described by a master architectural and social historian like Arthur Hart, are now beginning to be appreciated by an ever-increasing number of people who support the concept of historic preservation as an important, sensible and necessary element in the life of a community.

Boise, like most cities in the inland American West, cannot boast of large numbers of old, significant buildings of high architectural merit. Nevertheless, the pioneer buildings that have been saved and the other later examples illustrated in *Historic Boise* provide a panorama of our aspirations, development, industry, religion, taste, and fashionable whims. In short, they are a snapshot of characteristic Americana important in their own right and too good to allow to be lost through carelessness or thoughtless greed.

It was the intention of the Boise City Historic Preservation Commission in first publishing this book to remind us that we do have this legacy and that it has value. There is little doubt that most of the present owners of these buildings and the owners of many other fine older structures in Boise would happily agree.

That there is heightened interest in local history and preservation is proved by the fact that *Historic Boise* is now in its fourth printing which, like the third, is sponsored by Historic Idaho, Inc., a non-profit venture organized by Barbara Hansen and Robert Aldridge, members of the city commission originally sponsoring the project. The corporation's recent book, with Arthur Hart as author, is *The Boiseans: At Home,* a series of entertaining vignettes of Boise social history linked with the houses and domestic lifestyles of an earlier time. All of the money earned by Historic Idaho, Inc. in these ventures is used for the benefit of historic preservation. These two little volumes are companion pieces. I urge the readers of this book also to obtain *The Boiseans: At Home* for a more intimate view of our lively recent past.

Charles F. Hummel, F.A.I.A.
November, 1993

Introduction

The Setting

Boise, Idaho is located on the edge of a northern sagebrush desert at the foot of mountains. It is watered by the Boise river and several creeks. Irrigation has given the city the character of an oasis for over a century. The foothills behind the city are dry, for even though they receive more rain and snow than the townsite itself, they are inclined toward the southern sun and prevailing winds which dry them out. Only near the summit of the Boise Front does enough snow accumulate to provide moisture for an evergreen forest and lush underbrush.

East of the city the prominent shape of a sandstone mesa called Table Rock recalls the geologic fact that this land was once under ancient seas. Fossil shells are found in this sandstone. Hot springs well up near its base. Successive benches of gravel on the south side of Boise river were left by the river over centuries of high and low flow and changes of course. Beyond the level areas of the benches sagebrush plains once stretched unbroken to the basaltic rim rocks of the Snake river, 30 miles to the south. Irrigated crops and housing developments now replace the sagebrush. Beyond the Snake the Owyhee mountains rise, blue in summer and shining white in winter.

4.
Hudson's Bay Company's Fort Boise, at the mouth of the Boise River, near Parma, was built in 1834 from large mud bricks made on the spot. A change in the course of the river has obliterated much of the site.

5.
The original plat of Boise City, drawn in July, 1863, showed a Main Street dividing 10 blocks. Each block had an alleyway and 12 lots 25 x 100 feet. H.C. Riggs, Pinckney Lugenbeel, John McClellan, and Cyrus Jacobs are prominent early names written on these lots.

6.
Arm Hincelin, a carriage painter, produced this earliest view of Boise City about the time it became the Capital in 1864. It shows Main Street looking east toward Table Rock. Most buildings appear to be wood or adobe, with brick ones conspicuous by contrast.

The Founding

The site was chosen for an army post in 1863, and the town started at the same time. The need felt by General George Wright, commander of the Pacific Coast district, was for "a military post at or near Fort Boise on the Snake River. The great necessity for a strong garrison in that quarter is daily becoming more apparent. In the very heart of the mining districts of the north and on a route by which vast emigration from the East approaches that country, a strong military post can afford protection to all against those wandering bands of Indians which infest that section, and maintain peace between races." The "Fort Boise" referred to by Wright was the old Hudson's Bay post at the mouth of Boise River, founded in 1834 and abandoned in 1855. When authorization to build a new army fort came from the War Department on January 14, 1863, Wright notified General Benjamin Alvord of the Oregon department to proceed, and narrowed down the location to "some forty miles east of the old fort up the Boise River, where wood, water, grass and cultivable land can be found."

Major Pinckney Lugenbeel of the 9th Infantry at Fort Vancouver was chosen by Alvord as the best man to lead the expedition "as he has had in the construction of Fort Colville and elsewhere much experience and is admirably qualified for the duty." General Wright agreed, calling him "very industrious, active, and economical, with much experience in planning and building."

4

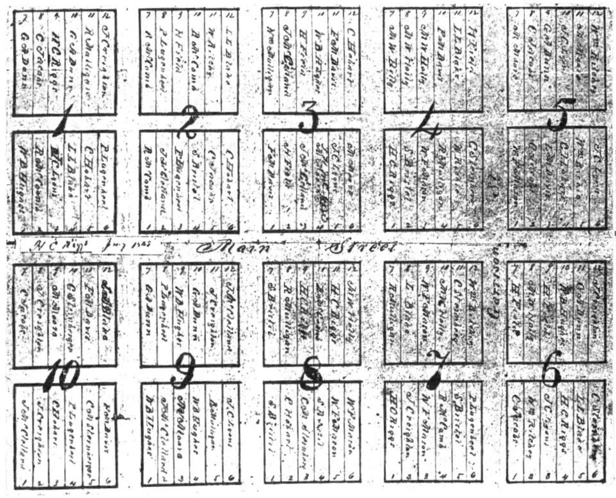

5

6

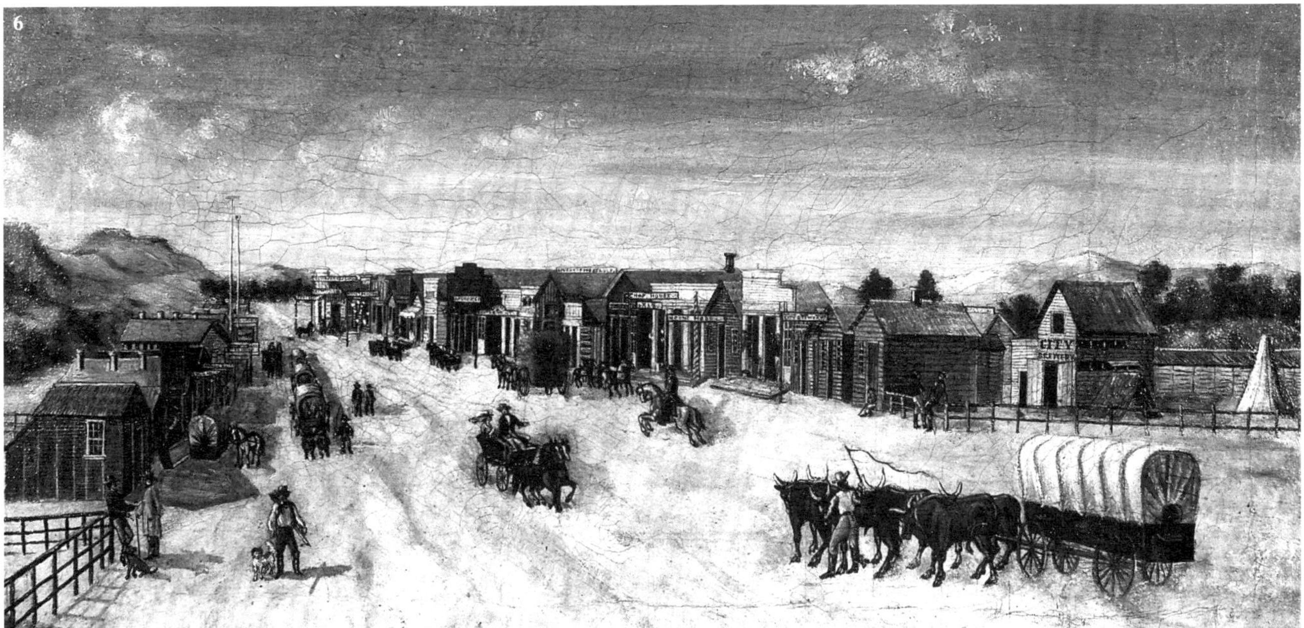

7

Lugenbeel's written orders stated that "the selection of the site is left entirely to your discretion, being satisfied that you will pay due regard to salubrity, military defense, and the protection of the frontier." He was further cautioned by Alvord as to "the necessity of great economy in the building of the temporary quarters for five companies which should be erected at the post."

On July 4, 1863, Lugenbeel chose the site for his fort. With the Boise Front at its back, Cottonwood Creek coming out of the hills to the east, and with sufficient elevation to command an unobstructed view in three directions, the spot was ideal. A few settlers already had crops growing without irrigation along the river. There was adequate grazing for livestock, and an abundant supply of sandstone for building purposes. The valley of Cottonwood Creek could be followed to a low summit, beyond which More's Creek drainage led to the booming Boise Basin Mines. The Oregon Trail , or Overland Road, ran along the first bench beyond Boise River, and emigrant trains were rolling along it in steady procession, as they had every summer since 1842.

On July 7, 1863, eight men met in a cabin belonging to Tom Davis and William L. Ritchey, who had started a ranch on the river that spring. They laid out a townsite between the river and the fort made up of five blocks on each side of a "Main Street." (The only other street named in the original plat is "Garrison St.", later to be called Sixth). The first shelters put up on Main street were either tents, or what were described a year later as "brush shanties."

7.
Major Pinckney Lugenbeel selected the site for the Army's Fort Boise. After supervising its construction he was transferred elsewhere.

8.
This earliest view of Fort Boise shows the flagpole flanked by cannons. The dry sagebrush eventually become a lush oasis, but to the early army garrison it was dusty and bleak. The Fort was redesignated as Boise Barracks in 1879 and continued as an active army post until 1912. The site became a Veterans Administration Hospital in 1920 and was placed on the National Register of Historic Places in 1972.

9.
The plat of the Boise City Original Townsite recorded by Mayor Prickett on November 25, 1867. This "official" survey replaced the first plat of 1863 and expanded the townsite from 10 to 140 numbered blocks with a double block reserved as the "Capitol Square." Block 35 was reserved for the Assay Office and Block 65 for the Court House. The original 10 blocks have the same numbers and the erratic numbering system of the blocks reflects the sequence of land claims after that.

8

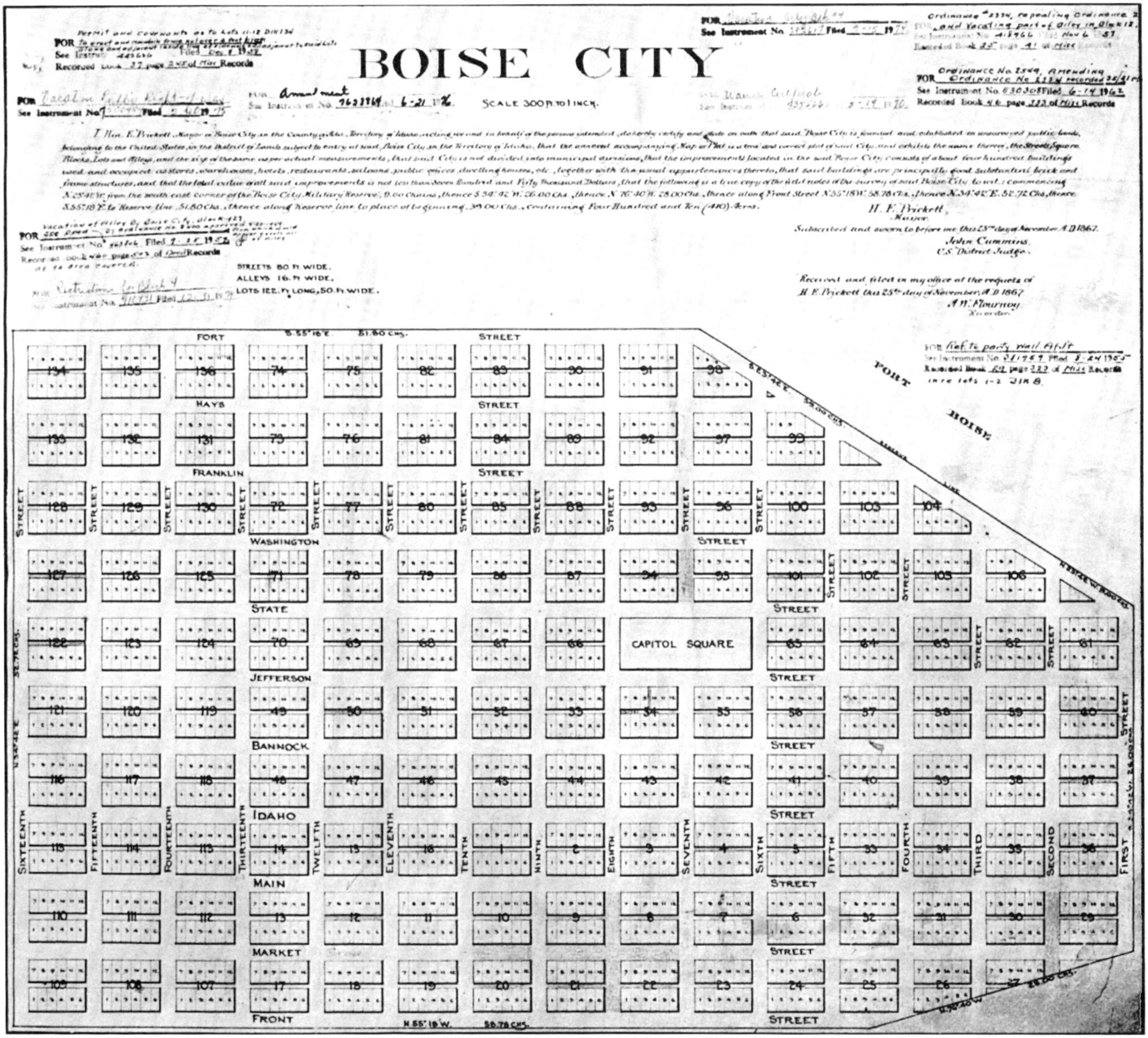

BOISE CITY
SCALE 300 ft. to 1 INCH.
STREETS 80 ft. WIDE.
ALLEYS 16 ft. WIDE.
LOTS 122 ft. LONG, 50 ft. WIDE.
H. E. Prickett
Mayor.
John Cummins
U.S. District Judge.
A.W. Flournoy
Recorder.
FORT STREET
HAYS STREET
FRANKLIN STREET
WASHINGTON STREET
STATE STREET
JEFFERSON STREET
BANNOCK STREET
IDAHO STREET
MAIN STREET
MARKET STREET
FRONT STREET
CAPITOL SQUARE
FORT BOISE
SIXTEENTH STREET
FIFTEENTH STREET
FOURTEENTH STREET
THIRTEENTH STREET
TWELFTH STREET
ELEVENTH STREET
TENTH STREET
NINTH STREET
EIGHTH STREET
SEVENTH STREET
SIXTH STREET
FIFTH STREET
FOURTH STREET
THIRD STREET
SECOND STREET
FIRST STREET

10.
This 1866 photograph of Boise City's Main Street has become a local classic. The dirt street is crowded with action – freight wagons, mule and ox teams, and false-gabled frontier architecture. The photographer was on top of a porch at Sixth and Main, looking west.

STAGE HOUSE
HOTEL

FROM THE
NEW MILL!
THE UNDERSIGNED are now prepared to furnish
Lumber in Quantities
to suit, both clear and common, in Boise City and Valley, or at the Mill, on Stewart's Gulch, ten miles from town. Bills promptly filled. Office at Jacob's & Co.'s store from 9 A. M. to 3 P. M.
Hand in your Orders.
PURVINE BROTHERS.
W. B. Hunter, Agent. fe28tf

11

The building types used in Boise City in its first years showed the strong influence of both local materials and the traditions settlers brought with them. A few pioneers had built log cabins in the valley in the spring of 1863 before the army arrived to establish the fort. The city's three surviving cabins of that year show the importance of Mississippi valley traditions; old photographs of others show the same structural methods.

The John O'Farrell cabin, now on Fort Street near Fifth, employs the steeple-notched technique. That of Isaac Coston, formerly located east of town and now in Julia Davis Park, has full-dovetail corners, and the Pierce cabin next door, originally near 5th and Main, has half-dovetail corners. All of these methods of corner notching, to secure a strong interlocking structure, had already been used for generations in the East when Boise's first cabins were put together.

Cottonwood logs, though not ideal because of their variable diameters and crookedness, were made useable by broad-axing the sides flat. The characteristic vertical chop marks of the broad-ax are still visible on the logs of Boise's 1863 cabins. The pine and fir trees on the mountain ridges to the north and east would have worked better, but they were too far away to tempt cabin builders, for whom temporary shelter was the objective. As soon as a sawmill could be set up, cabins were abandoned for real board houses, however modest. (It would always be easier to cut timber several miles up the Boise river and float it down to the mills than to climb the Boise front for it, however, and the Douglas fir and Ponderosa pine woods visible from the city are largely intact today, as part of the Boise National Forest.)

At least one early store building used cottonwood logs in a different way. When Crawford & Slocum's 1863 store was torn down in March, 1874, the Statesman described it as follows: "The only lumber in the building is in the roof boards six inches wide on which the shingles are nailed. . . It is built of small cottonwood poles set in the ground endways. The building never was honored with a floor, other than the ground. It has an excellent shingle roof and stands as firm as ever."

From this account that both boards and shingles were used in 1863, it is evident that a sawmill was built almost at once. Certainly by the summer of 1864, when the Idaho Tri-Weekly Statesman began publication, there were mills up-river supplying the building boom in Idaho's newest metropolis. On August 16, 1864, the Statesman noted that "Wagon loads of lumber are arriving every day from the saw mills for building purposes." A. H. Robie & C. S. Bush were the proprietors of one of these mills. In 1865, Alexander Rossi, who had worked for Robie in Lewiston in 1861 and in Idaho City in 1862, came to Boise to take Bush's place in the partnership. Mills operated by Rossi would supply the city with lumber into the 20th century.

11.
Lumber for building purposes was readily available at an early date, as this 1865 ad from the Idaho Tri-Weekly Statesman shows.

12.
John O'Farrell, a native of County Tyrone, Ireland, built this log cabin in the summer of 1863. Fathers Mesplie and Poulin conducted Roman Catholic services here after they were recognized as priests by Mrs. O'Farrell as they rode past on their way to Oregon. Thereafter, Father Mesplie ministered regularly to the Catholics of Fort Boise and Boise City. This view of the O'Farrell cabin was made before a protective shed was built over it.

13.
Full-dovetail notching provided a tightly locked log cabin corner. This is a detail of the Isaac N. Coston cabin in Pioneer Village.

14.
Half-dovetail corner notching worked nearly as well and was simpler to make. Pierce cabin, Pioneer Village.

15.
Steeple notching allowed the water to drain out of the interlocked corners, reducing the chance of wet rot. O'Farrell cabin, Fort Street.

12

13

14

15

16

Board and batten buildings, or simply vertical board buildings with no studs or framing, were often built in the sixties. Horizontal boards at top and bottom held together these inch-thick walls, which were covered with muslin on the inside and wallpapered. An 1872 addition to the Mayor Thomas E. Logan house, removed in 1971, was constructed in this fashion, with clapboards added to the outside.

Adobe buildings were also put up almost at once, an expedient which reflected the high cost of lumber, fire hazards, and the traditions of the Southwest, where sun-dried mud-brick had been used for centuries. About half of the first settlers in Boise valley had been in California before coming to Idaho, and some of them were Mexicans. The army, too, had frequently built of adobe in its Western posts. Some of the artisans in Lugenbeel's detachment had probably worked with it before. Adobe was used in the Northwest in fur trade and missionary days in a variety of ways. The Hudson's Bay Company Fort Boise, established in 1834 at the mouth of Boise River on the Snake, was built of large slab-like adobes measuring 9.5 x 4.5 x 2.75 inches, and Fort Hall, 300 miles upriver, was of similar construction.

The Mayor Thomas E. Logan house, formerly located on the east side of Sixth street between Main and Grove, and now in Julia Davis Park, was built of adobe bricks made on site in about 1865. These adobes are rich brown in color, made of river bottom topsoil with the rootlets of native vegetation scattered through them. The house was given a coat of barn red oil-base paint soon after its completion. Periodic paintings over the past century have preserved the structure remarkably well, enabling it to withstand a move of more than half a mile in 1971 without sustaining even a crack in the wall fabric.

Cyrus Jacobs' 1863 adobe store building at the southwest corner of Seventh and Main was one of the city's first. He tore it down in 1865 and replaced it with a brick structure with a three-arched front. However, other 1863 buildings of adobe were repaired in May, 1865, and the method described by the Idaho Tri-Weekly Statesman: "The adobe buildings which were at first the only resort of the settlers of Boise City, have in most cases been found to answer nearly as well as brick, the greatest difficulty being from moisture at the bottom of the walls. To remedy this cut stone is being placed under most of them."

As Boise City grew, great pride was taken in so-called "fire-proof" buildings. Merchants who had built adobe stores referred to them in ads as "fireproof brick", and, in deference to its advertisers, the early Tri-weekly Statesman rarely made the distinction in news stories, either. By September, 1864, John Brown and Charles May had a brick kiln in operation between Third and Fourth streets on Main. The Statesman noted that "Messrs May & Brown have a kiln

16.
Thomas E. Logan came to Boise in 1864. He served as postmaster and was elected Mayor four times in the 1870s.

17.
The adobe Mayor Thomas E. Logan house, 1865, was moved from Sixth and Grove in 1971 to its present location in Pioneer Village. Although adobe buidings were common in Boise in the 1860s, only the Logan House survives. This is because it was protected with a red oil-base paint soon after its construction.

18.
The "Stone Jug" was the center of Idaho government in territorial days. The site is now the Old Telephone Building at 609 Main Street.

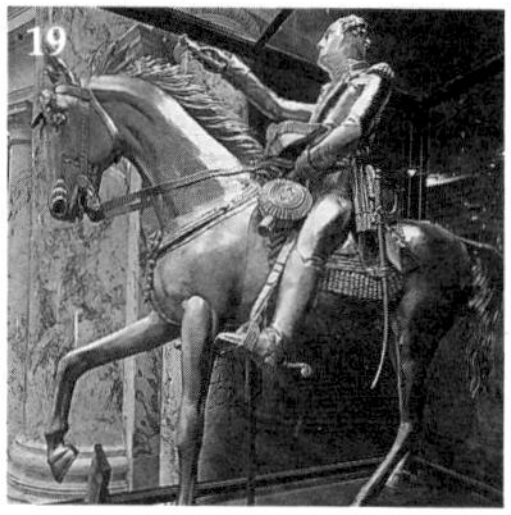

19.
Charles Ostner's statue of George Washington in the Capitol rotunda. It first stood outside on a stone pedestal at the west side of the Territorial Capitol and later on the east side of the State Capitol.

of one hundred and fifty thousand brick just burned, which are now ready for use . . . The kiln is nearly all contracted for, and the owners of the yard are going to put up another immediately."

Charles May, an Englishman, had come from Walla Walla in 1863 to help the army build the first stone structures at Fort Boise. The Quartermaster building, still standing, bears the inscription "September 1st, 1864." May was descended from generations of stonemasons in his native England and would work on important buildings throughout the West in later years.

There is one extant 1864 dwelling in Boise. It is the Cyrus Jacobs house at 607 Grove Street. This fired-brick building is on the National Register of Historic Places. Another historic brick structure of 1864, torn down in 1894, was B. M. Durell's general store and commission house at the southeast corner of Eighth and Main. Durell, who would be one of the founders of the First National Bank of Idaho in 1867, carried on assaying and banking operations in this building along with his other activities. He operated a branch in Ruby City (later replaced by Silver City) under the direction of C. W. Moore, who would eventually make Boise architectural history himself. Durell's building, which had iron fire doors imported from San Francisco, was later used by Twitchell & Moody as a hardware and tin shop, and was taken over in 1873 by Frank R. Coffin, a young employee in the firm. Coffin would build the Pioneer block on that corner in 1894 (later removed by Urban Renewal) and a Queen Anne mansion on Grove Street in 1891.

One architectural type among the city's store buildings deserves special note, since it was a standard in towns of the 1850s and '60s throughout the West. Cyrus Jacobs' 1865 store and the 1867 First National Bank were classic examples of the one-story brick commercial building with three-arched openings still to be seen in California gold rush mining camps and in Jacksonville, Oregon. Although none would survive in Boise, Idaho City has several, and later examples are conspicuous in Genessee in the Palouse country of North Idaho.

Sandstone, found in abundance all along the foothills north and east of town, was used at the Fort and in downtown buildings starting in 1864. Territorial Secretary E. J. Curtis built in 1868 what would be a landmark for a generation. The "Stone Jug", as it was lovingly called by old-timers, served as Curtis' law office and the seat of Idaho government during the many years when Curtis was acting governor. (A capitol would not be built until 1886.) Charles Ostner, the pioneer artist who carved the equestrian George Washington now in the Statehouse, came to town to present the statue to the people of Idaho Territory in January, 1869. He stayed on to carve the decorative elements on the Stone Jug and to do tombstones and other fancy work in stone. Two examples are in the collections of the Idaho Historical Society, along with paintings and wood carvings. John Broadbent built

20.
The Quartermaster Building at Fort Boise is one of two sandstone buildings at the Fort built in the 1860s. The other is Building No. 1 – the Commandant's House – still used as a residence.

21.
The Cyrus Jacobs house at 607 Grove Street dates from 1864. Jacobs, a city founder and early merchant, miller, and meat packer was famous for producting a rye whiskey called Jacobs' Best.

22.
Cy Jacobs' store stood on the southwest corner of Main and Seventh Streets. He started business there in July, 1863, in a tent.

23.
The 1864 adobe store on the southeast corner of Eighth and Main built by B.M. Durrell. He ran a general merchandise, assaying, and banking business there. Frank Coffin made it into a tin shop and hosted this party of pioneers before starting the Pioneer Building in 1894.

20

21

22

WHOLESALE LIQUOR DEALER
C. JACOBS.

23

STOVES. TIN-SHOP.
FRANK R. COFFIN & BRO.

24

a new stone store in April, May and June, 1869, which the Statesman called "a superior piece of architecture" and "the most handsome work of the kind in the Territory."

Boise had over 400 buildings at the end of the Sixties, of which 24 were brick and 8 were stone. The largest frame buildings, in what was still largely a wooden town, were two hotels, a church, and a lodge hall. The Overland House, built in 1864, was a California-inspired structure with a long second story porch, reminiscent of Spanish colonial types still standing in Monterey. It had a frontage of 75 feet on Eighth and 50 feet on Main, and would be the focal point of town life until torn down in 1904 to make way for the Eastman building. Hart's Exchange, somewhat larger, was built in 1866 at the southeast corner of Seventh and Idaho streets, where city hall now stands. It, too, had a two-story verandah, but its higher gables gave it a character that was more New England than Spanish.

St. Michael's Episcopal church was also completed in 1866. This neat white Gothic revival building, now called Christ Chapel, still stands in a new location on the campus of Boise State University near the Broadway bridge. Gothic was considered the only fitting style for Christian worship at the time, replacing the Greek revival which had dominated American architecture before the Civil war. A Boise building which did have classical characteristics was the Good Templars' Hall, completed in 1870 near the corner of Sixth and Main. Constructed as a meeting place for the temperance lodge, then attracting a wide following, this two-story hall also served as a theater, roller skating rink, bowling alley, and rented meeting space for the legislature in its 40 years of existence.

In the fall of 1863, Boise City had 725 people. A year later the number had more than doubled to 1,658. since 90 per cent of Idaho's population was now located in the southern part of the territory, there was an active push by Boise to secure the capital from Lewiston, which had dwindled from 414 in 1863 to 359 in 1864. The second legislature, meeting in Lewiston, gave the capital to Boise on December 24, 1864 — an action that Lewiston failed to check in a series of maneuvers that a leading historian calls "one of the most hilarious chapters in the long Idaho story."

Boise's economic base was sound, despite the declining fortunes of nearby mining communities which lost much of their population after 1866. The first rush to a new gold country always drew far more people than it could support, but as the supply and transportation center of a large and diversified region, Boise remained a fairly stable city. The continued growth of quartz mining, improved methods of placering, and above all the increase in farming and ranching kept Boise a commercial center. The first federal census in Boise City in 1870 revealed a population of about 1000, indicating that the decline in mining had its effect there, too.

24.
Hart's Exchange was one of Boise City's earliest hostelries. It stood where City Hall is today. This ad appeared in 1868.

25.
Hart's Exchange, later the Central Hotel, was a typical frontier hotel. The Territorial Legislature rented it for sessions before there was a capitol.

26.
The Good Templars' Hall was the city's largest meeting place for many years. It was one of the few buildings in Boise to show Greek Revival characteristics, such as the quoins at the corners of the facade. This photo was taken on the Fourth of July.

27.
The famous Overland House was built at Eighth and Main in 1864. Its architectural form was an echo of early California.

28.
The Overland House was remodeled and enlarged more than once. The roofline had changed dramatically by the 1890s when this photograph was taken.

25

26

27

28

29.
Christ Chapel's white Gothic Revival delicacy has graced the city since 1866. Now in its third location, on Broadway next to the Boise River, this building was preserved through the efforts of the Idaho Statesman and the Sons and Daughters of Idaho Pioneers.

31

1802

1309

The city of the Sixties had a large number of its people living in tents or shacks. In the Seventies more substantial houses with architectural pretensions were built, especially along Grove street, next south of Main. Elliott's 1884 *History of Idaho Territory,* published in San Francisco, gives us our best idea of these fine houses and the growing architectural pride they embodied. The artist's drawings also suggest the increased importance of trees and landscaping.

A number of styles were represented on Grove street, but most were reflections of A. J. Downing's *The Architecture of Country Houses,* a widely read and influential book on picturesque architecture published first in 1850 and reissued 8 times by 1866. Druggist William Nye's house was a fine example of the "cottage ornee," a variant of the Gothic revival domestic style which had rich jig-sawed wooden ornament but virtually no authentic Gothic forms. The Milton Kelly and John Lemp houses were much plainer, displaying only the fancy cut-out "barge boards" of Gothic revival cottages. Lafayette Cartee added a large two-story addition to his house near Fourth and Grove in 1875, making it the most impressive wooden dwelling on the street. Elliott's history labeled it a "villa," using the vocabulary of Downing's books for such structures that were larger than a "cottage". Band-saw "gingerbread" covered this impressive building, not torn down until 1952. Cartee, who was Surveyor General of Idaho in territorial days, also ran the Grove Street Nursery and was a pioneer introducer of rare horticultural varieties to the city. He was also active in all civic projects, including the formation of the city's first fire department in 1876, of which he was elected president.

The grandest Grove street house of the decade was built in 1879 by C. W. Moore of the First National Bank. Later known as the DeLamar Hotel, this brick mansard-roofed dwelling with its bay windows and elegant iron roof-cresting was the largest and most expensive house built in Idaho at that time. Of special architectural interest is the number of mail-order elements incorporated into the house. When the building was demolished in 1972, the Idaho Historical Society salvaged the walnut newel post and balustrade from the front stairway, door hardware, plaster ceiling rosettes, roof brackets, portions of cresting, and an entire bay window — all manufactured in the East, ordered from a catalog, and shipped to Boise. Much of this material is on display today in the State Museum.

Two important public buildings were built in Boise at the beginning of the Seventies. A territorial penitentiary was completed in 1870 at the foot of Table Rock, east of the city. The walls of this stone structure can still be seen in the National Register Old Penitentiary historic district, with a number of larger and more impressive buildings of the Nineties. It was first modified architecturally and then gutted by fire in a 1972 prison riot.

31.
These engravings, from the mail order catalog of Iowa manufacturer M.A. Disbrow, show elements used in Boise's C.W. Moore house of 1879.

32.
Druggist William Nye's house was an especially rich example of the Gothic Revival cottage in wood – more imaginative than authentic.

33.
C.W. Moore's mansion at Eighth and Grove was Idaho's most elegant mansard style dwelling. The bay window at right is in the State Museum.

34.
Begun in 1870, the Old Idaho Penitentiary was built of local sandstone quarried by the inmates. The first building was burned in a 1972 prison riot.

32

33

34

35

The 1872 United States Assay Office, on the other hand, is in a nearly perfect state of preservation. A. B. Mullet, most prolific of U.S. Treasury Department supervising architects, was responsible for its design. It is an Italianate cube with a cupola on top, achieving monumentality through its proportions and the excellent sandstone masonry employed. Millions of dollars in gold and silver passed through the Assay Office between 1872 and 1933, when it was turned over to the U.S. Forest Service as a district headquarters. In 1973 it was conveyed to the State and the care of the Idaho Historical Society. It houses a museum of western rocks and the offices of the State Archaeologist, and is a popular picnic spot due to its full city block of lawn and stately trees.

Of the dozen or more brick commercial structures built on Main street in the Seventies only one survives.It is Joseph Perrault's building on the southeast corner of Seventh and Main, built in 1879 to house a harness and saddle shop. A stone front on Main was later replaced by a new stone facing which covers half of the Seventh (Capitol Boulevard) side as well. House of Louie, a Chinese restaurant in the southern half of the building, still exhibits the original handsome brick arches over its windows. This building later had a two-story wooden verandah for a time, on the Seventh street side.

The Methodists, Boise's largest church denomination in the Seventies, held ardently evangelistic tent meetings throughout the Territory. They built the first brick church in town in 1876. It was a tall-towered Gothic revival building on the corner later occupied by the Hotel Boise. Although designed by Captain Griffin, a contractor, it was a good reproduction of the popular church style of the day.

The biggest change in the city's character in the Seventies was its transformation into a "city of trees," and, along with its handsome buildings, this name was to be Boise's pride thereafter. "The big ditch back of town is full of water," wrote the Statesman in May, 1871. "Boise City now stands on an artificial island. There are a few hundred acres in here now that can be made to bloom as the Garden of Eden . . . let the householders now plant things and beautify their homes . . .". This was but one of dozens of such admonitions Editor James S. Reynolds was to give his readers in the early years when the little town in the sagebrush was struggling to get shade and fruit trees established. In a facetious reference to Salt Lake City, Reynolds concluded another such article with "Boise will ere long rival her great wicked but beautiful sister of the plains". Like the Mormon capital, Boise ran streams of water along her dusty streets in summer, enhancing the oasis character she sought.

The Grove street ditch, which ran along the north side of this pleasant residential thoroughfare, became noted in the years that followed for its big wooden water wheels. Their function was to lift water to the land above the ditch. Grove street itself had the city's first tall over-arching elms, and the lushness of Cartee's nursery at its upper end made the name appropriate.

35.
Bricklaying was done by master craftsmen when this window was framed. It can be seen at the House of Louie restaurant on Capitol Boulevard.

36.
The United States Assay Office at 210 Main Street was designed in the office of A.B. Mullet, Chief Architect of the Treasury Department. Mullet probably designed more public buildings than any man in history.

37.
The 1874 brick First Methodist Church stood at Eighth and Bannock where the Hotel Boise was later built.

38.
This detail from an early oil painting shows the water wheels which once lined Grove Street. They lifted water to the higher ground north of the ditch.

39.
Building No. 4, at Fort Boise, shows a brick addition of the 1870s to a stone house of the 1860s.

36

37

38

39

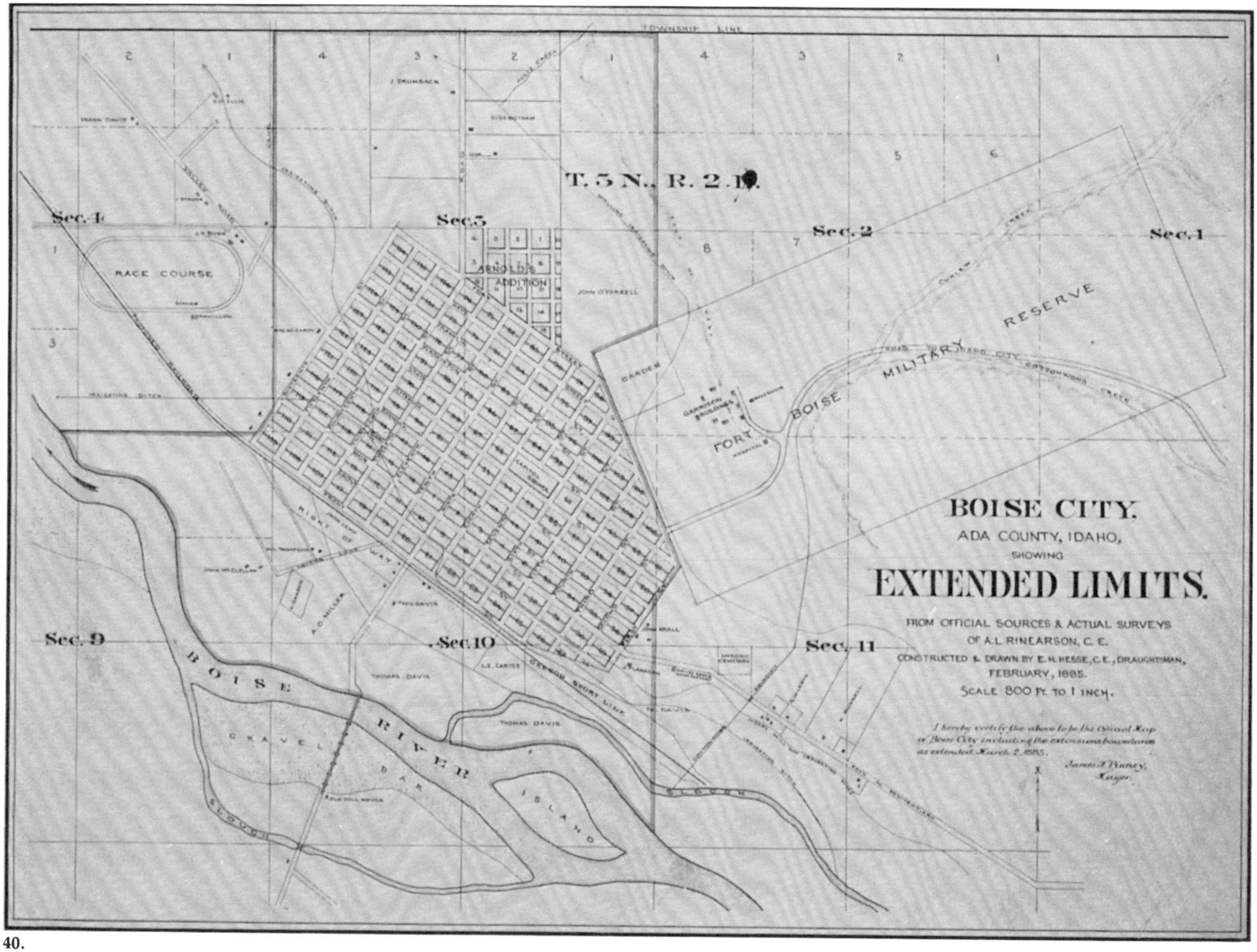

40.

This 1885 City Map was certified by Mayor James A. Pinney as official. It contains a great deal of information of historic interest, including land ownership, location of outlying buildings, canals, and the "proposed railroad" right of way not used until 9 years later. South of Boise River, which changed courses often through the years, can be seen a large "gravel bar" where the Boise State campus is today.

41.
Richardsonian Romanesque at its best is demonstrated by the Boise City National Bank (later Simplot) building at Eighth and Idaho. The rusticated local sandstone gives the walls a "quilted" look.

42.
Galvanized iron cornices were added to many downtown buildings after the railroad came in 1887. This cornice was on a building which stood where the Bank of Idaho is today.

The great event for the city in the Eighties was the completion of the Oregon Short Line railroad, although its location 15 miles south of town was a bitter disappointment. Since her merchants and government leaders had worked hard for more than a decade to secure a railroad through Boise City and across southern Idaho, following the Oregon Trail, they resented the creation of the upstart new towns of Kuna, Nampa, and Caldwell on the main line. Actually, the growth of these places was to enhance Boise's prosperity in the long run, since it continued to be the wholesale center of the region. In 1887, a branch line from Nampa to Boise was completed which served the city until the main line was brought through Boise in 1925.

Boise had already benefitted from the completion of the transcontinental railroad across Utah and Nevada in 1869. Over the years when Boise merchants supplied the mining camps of Boise Basin, and Owyhee and Alturas counties, freight teams hauled thousands of tons of supplies from Kelton, Utah, over what was known as the Kelton road, to warehouses in Boise for transshipment to the smaller towns later.

The railroad conferred no architectural distinction on the town at first, since its depot on the bench was a primitive board and batten structure, but it did make available to local builders products not seen in Boise City before. Galvanized iron made its impact on the city's appearance as soon as the railroad came, and many wooden structures were roofed or sided in the corrugated sheets to increase their fire resistance. The city council ruled that these buildings were still not in compliance with the 1881 fire district ordinance, however, which mandated brick or stone construction. Most galvanized iron in the center of town after this ruling was decorative. Whole sheet iron cornices and store fronts were imported from St. Louis and other midwest cities, making "style" available at low cost to merchants in a town without trained architects. The 19th century loved ornament, and a number of Boise commercial buildings of the late Eighties and early Nineties used a galvanized iron and zinc cornice to achieve effects of great richness. Three examples from the south side of Main were salvaged by the Historical Society when Boise's redevelopment project took them down in the 1970s. The Bouquet Bar, Purcell's Western clothing store, and Singer's loan building all had imported cornices which reproduced, in stamped and soldered sheet iron, classic architectural motifs designed for carved stone.

Cast iron was also in great vogue in the Eighties, but Boise produced its own. The foundries needed in most mining districts for manufacture and repair of the heavy castings used in steam engines, pumps, and stamp mills could easily produce architectural castings when needed. The introduction of cast iron pilasters and columns did not come locally until 1888, even though the city had had a foundry since June of 1865. Among the buildings which added new iron fronts and plate glass windows in the spring of 1888 were D. Falk & Bro., Ed Shainwald, Epstein & Logan, and James A. Pinney.

43.
A simple board and batten shack was Boise City's first depot. It stood on the "bench" east of the present location.

44.
In 1894 the trains came downtown along Front Street to a handsome new station. The locomotives were still classic 1860s "diamond stackers." This station stood on the site of the present U.P. freight office between Ninth and Tenth.

45.
In 1889, Boise City still had a dirt Main Street, even though most of the buildings were now of brick. This view, from Eighth Street looking East, shows Nye's drug store and Falk's store at left. Coffin's tin shop at right, and the fire hall tower in the distance. Plate glass and iron fronts were added to many of these buildings.

43

44

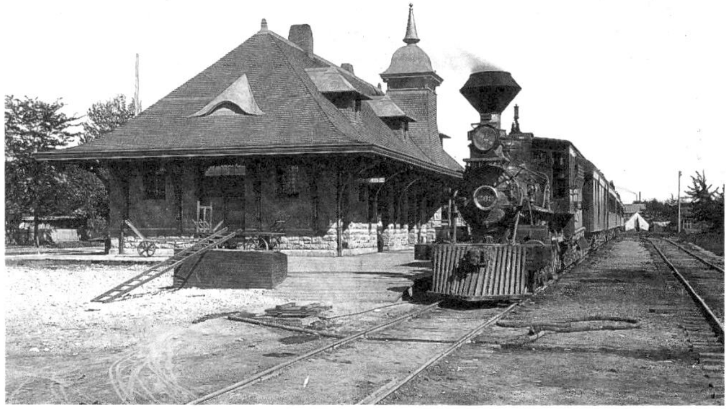

45

Peter Sonna's 1888 two story brick building at the corner of Ninth and Main was designed to be an iron and glass front from the beginning. It also had elegant iron roof-cresting. S. C. Torrence's Boise City Foundry, which had been in operation since 1883, "ran out 2500 pounds of casting for Sonna's building. . ."in window weights alone, and also did the columns which still support part of this building behind the new brick front added in its 1976 remodeling.

The Statesman wondered on April 8, 1888, "Where will this plate glass craze end?". The railroad was responsible for the availability of large sheets of plate glass for the first time, and the cast iron and glass formed a new structural system for store fronts, which allowed larger displays and let in more light. Other older buildings added the new fronts as well — the drugstore on the northeast corner of Eighth and Main (first Nye's, then Ridenbaugh's) in July 1889, and Levi's at Fifth and Idaho in October, 1891.

Boise got a three story brick building in 1881 when John Lemp completed a big structure on the south side of Main between Eighth and Ninth, housing the Capital Hotel and several stores. Four other large brick buildings would be built before the decade was out. The Territorial Capital (1886), Central School (1883), and the Ada County Courthouse (1881) made an impressive triumvirate at Capitol Square — a sagebrush lot which had been vacant from the town's beginning awaiting public buildings. The "Norman" Romanesque Capitol was from the designs of E. E. Myers, a Detroit architect who won a competition over other architects invited to submit drawings. Central School was a mansard-roofed structure with a cupola and the courthouse was Italianate with a cupola. "The public buildings located in the city are numerous, and some of them imposing and ornamental structures," wrote Portland's *The West Shore* magazine in October, 1885, while the capitol was being built. It characterized the new capitol as "splendid and architecturally beautiful," and the school as "handsome", with "few rivals . . . on the Pacific coast." The I.O.O.F. Hall (1889), described later, was the decade's other large brick building.

The same article referred to the city's residential architecture as follows: "There are many very handsome two and three-store frame and brick dwellings that would reflect credit upon a much older and larger town." One of these was Coffin brothers' on Grove street, built in 1882. It had 12 rooms — 5 with bath and pantry on the first floor and 7 on the upper floor. A landmark house which survived until the 1950s was Judge H. E. Prickett's brick mansard style dwelling on the southeast corner of Third and Main, across from the Assay office. When the judge moved his family into the new home on January 16, 1884, the Statesman said "This is the most stylish, and probably the most expensive residence in the city." Prickett had the distinction of serving as Boise's first mayor when city government was formed on November 18, 1867.

46.
James H. Hawley was a famous frontier lawyer who served both as Mayor of Boise and Governor of Idaho.

47.
Peter Sonna's 1888 building at Ninth and Main had an opera house upstairs and hardware store downstairs.

48.
Judge H.E. Prickett was Boise's first Mayor. He built this ornate mansard-roofed house in 1884. The house was later bought by Governor Hawley.

49.
This 1890 engraving shows Boise's pride and joy: Central School, Territorial Capitol and Courthouse. The present Capitol occupies the site of the Central School and Territorial Capitol. The present Courthouse is on the same site as the original.

47

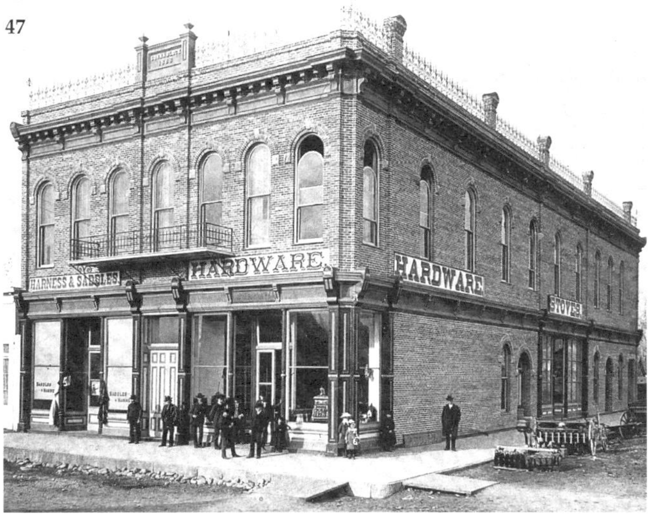

48

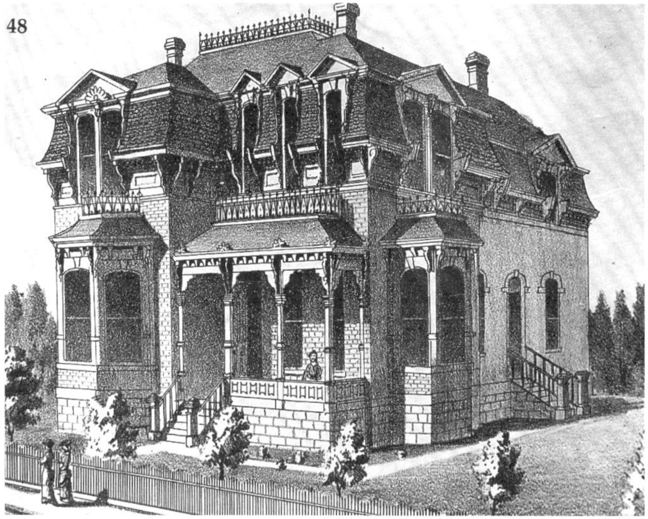

49

J. W. Daniels served as Superintendant of Schools in Boise for many years, devoting himself assiduously to cultural leadership for the community. It is not surprising, therefore, that he should build a house of exceptional character. Although it has long been gone from the scene, one fine photograph in the collection of the Idaho Historical Society shows it to have been a dramatic example of the towered "stick style," with Eastlake decoration. The "stick" tendency in American wooden architecture has recurred periodically for more than a century. The most notable symptom of stick style is an emphasis upon the frame of the house, often with an exaggereated skeletal or half-timbered look. The custom in those days was to paint buildings in contrasting colors, greatly enhancing this effect. Charles Eastlake, author of *Hints on Household Taste,* had his greatest influence on the furniture of the Seventies and Eighties, but architecture also used his decorative ideas, as Daniels' house shows. The Statesman, in its role as critic of local architecture, defended Daniels' house against "some who think it too fanciful" by noting that "the tower adds to its beauty. They are becoming quite common in the prevailing architecture of the East."

R. Z. Johnson, who had been a successful lawyer in Silver City for many years, moved to Boise and built the handsome temple-like law office at 112 North Sixth Street in 1885. Although Greek revival in overall form, the three slender wooden columns are anti-classical in character — a reflection of the prevailing taste for cast iron at the time. Johnson had one of the territory's finest law libraries, and the impressive leather-bound volumes still line the walls of an interior remarkably unchanged after nearly a century.

W. W. Goodrich, a civil engineer from New York, who styled himself "architect" rather than simply contractor or builder, gave public lectures and wrote a series of articles on art and other cultural subjects for the Statesman in 1882. None of the buildings he designed in the city survived. Boise was probably too small to support a specialist in architectural design, and Goodrich left after two years. At the end of the decade, however, James King arrived from West Virginia and enjoyed a good patronage for 10 years. Although he designed one building finished in 1889, we shall discuss his career in the next section.

The arrival of the Idaho Central in 1887, the achievement of statehood on July 3, 1890, and the building of the New York Canal heralded a new era for the Capital City. Aware of its importance, and optimistic about the future, Boise began to build at an unprecedented rate in the Nineties. The population nearly doubled in 1890 alone, from about 2000 to 4000, and an agressive Board of Trade worked hard to attract people and business. Two architects dominated major construction in the first half of the decade, their projects carrying through to completion even after the panic of 1893 had chilled development in most other places.

50.
The Eastlake style in Boise architecture was best represented by School Superintendent J.W. Daniel's towered castle. It could also be considered "stick style."

51.
R.Z. Johnson's 1885 law office on Sixth Street is one of the City's little gems. Its slender wooden porch posts imitated newly-fashionable cast iron.

52.
The verandah across the front of the Star Rooming House at 512 Idaho Street gives it the character of a classic western movie set. It was used as a rooming house by the Boise Basque community. The gate in the foreground led to a pelota court at the rear.

53.
This double house at 1718 North 9th Street is a restrained wooden structure of about 1890. The fancy cut shingles in the gable suggest Queen Anne, but the symmetrical form is more Classical.

50

51

52

53

James King

James King, who arrived from Huntington, West Virginia in 1888, began his Boise career with two large downtown buildings next door to each other on Eighth street. His Odd Fellows hall was completed before 1889 was over. It was a narrow three story brick building with galvanized iron trim, housing ground-floor stores and space for offices upstairs in addition to the lodge hall itself. In 1890, the stone Romanesque revival Boise City National Bank building at the corner of Eighth and Idaho was designed, obviously modeled after H. H. Richardson's 1887 Marshal Field store in Chicago. Originally three stories high with a corner doorway, this building later had extensive additions and remodeling by Tourtellotte & Hummel after the turn of the century — changes which improved its proportions and enhanced its Richardsonian character. Most conspicuous was a fourth story culminating in fortress-like crenellations. Later known as the Simplot Building, this outstanding structure has been recognized by both the National Register of Historic Places and the Historic American Buildings Survey.

Romanesque revival buildings were popular all over America after Richardson led the way, beginning with his great Trinity Church, Boston, 1872, and culminating in the Marshal Field store, completed in 1887 after the architect's death. The Romanesque style of the early middle ages, upon which the revival was based, had massive walls, round arches, and often used rusticated stone (finished at the joints, but rough-textured and bulging on the surfaces.) The capitals of the thick Romanesque columns were highly stylized, often weaving plant forms into flattened patterns. Boise has several good examples.

King designed the 1893 Administration building at the Old Idaho Penitentiary — also a National Register site. Here he used Romanesque forms to create a powerful square building with a cathedral-like tower. It has crenellations around its parapet and another Romanesque feature in its big round-arched main entry.

In 1891 Peter Sonna extended his 1888 hardware building westward along Main, although he allowed King to design in a new brick format unlike the original at the corner of Ninth, which had round-arched second story windows for an opera house and ornate cast iron cresting. The addition, and a later one by W. S. Campbell in 1894, were more straighforward brick commercial blocks with rectangular upstairs windows. (The old building would later be remodeled to match King's addition, eliminating the opera house.)

The French chateau was eclectic designer King's inspiration for two other Boise buildings. In 1891 he designed a brick mansion with a diagonally set square corner towner for banker C. W. Moore at Walnut and Warm Springs Avenue. This house has the distinction, in addition to its architecture, of being the first in the United States heated with natural hot water. Boise's geothermal development of 1891-92 coincided with the building of this house for Moore, who was also one of the developers of the hot water systems.

54.
James King's Oddfellows Hall and Boise City National Bank buildings were an imposing addition to Eighth Street, 1889-92. The bank later acquired a fourth floor which improved its appearance greatly as seen in the view on page 29.

55.
The Administration Building at the Old Idaho Penitentiary was designed by James King in a rugged Romanesque style which makes it fortress-like – not inappropriate to the situation.

56.
The Moore-Cunningham house at Walnut and Warm Springs is King's only surviving French Chateau. Recently restored, it is one of the most admired houses on the Avenue.

57.
King's Idaho Soldiers' Home was changed from a Chateau into a Moorish Palace when J.E. Tourtellotte rebuilt it after a fire in 1900.

54

55

56

57

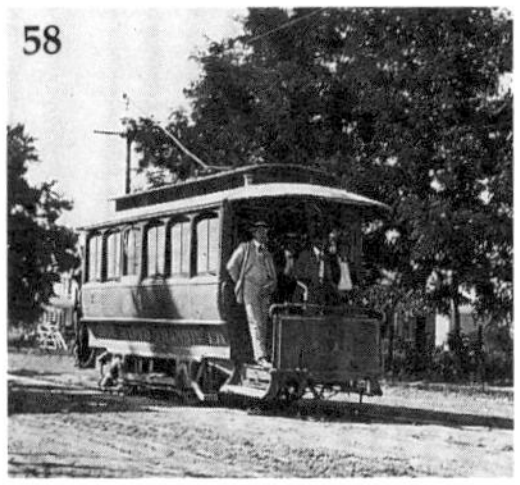

King's other chateau design was for the Idaho Soldiers Home, completed in 1894. When the original French-castle roof burned off in October, 1900, John E. Tourtellotte re-designed the structure in Moorish revival with a big onion dome in the center and smaller ones capping the corner turrets. It was indeed a romantic age.

The Queen Anne style swept the country in the 1880s, but Boise really got into the fad in the 1890s. Architect King designed one of the most impressive Queen Anne castles of the time for Boise capitalist William H. Ridenbaugh. His Boise Avenue house was a tall and complicated wooden structure with the typical characteristics of the style: a tall tower, porches at several levels, a wide wrap-around verandah, fancy cut shingles and "gingerbread" ornament produced by band saw and lathe. King also designed the original "Episcopal rectory" at the north-east corner of Idaho and Second streets. This "commodious wooden structure two stories high" was later enlarged to three stores to become the present "Bishops' House", relocated to the Old Idaho Penitentiary in 1976.

In 1896, Selden B. Kingsbury, a prominent Boise attorney, decided to join the rush to fashionable Warm Springs Avenue. He commissioned James King to design the big stone and shingle house at 1225 Warm Springs. It was one of only three houses pictured in Johnson's 1899 History of Idaho, pointing up the esteem in which it was held at the time.

John C. Paulsen

In the short time he was in Boise, German-trained John C. Paulsen of Helena, Montana, had a profound impact on the architectural character of the city. Paulsen designed, for the hot water company, one of the most exotic and spectacular buildings the city has ever had — the great Natatorium at the end of Warm Springs Avenue. Moorish in style, with two six-story towers, the "Nat" housed a swimming pool 125 feet long, a dining room, club rooms, saloon, dance floor, and a variety of card rooms, tea rooms, and baths. Wooden truss arches, 80 feet in diameter, enclosed the huge central space, which had a mezzanine running around the warm water pool and an artificial waterfall cascading down a rustic stone diving platform. The room was even used for Governors' inaugural balls by flooring over the swimming pool.

The street car system was developed at the same time, making it possible for patrons of the "Nat" to ride Boise Rapid Transit Company's little cars out Warm Springs Avenue for a nickel.

The Moorish revival was one of a number of 19th century romantic styles which harked back to earlier times and places. Key-hole-shaped arches were the single feature which set off the Moorish style from other "gingerbread" styles of the day, and the all wooden "Nat" managed to be exotic in appearance without being directly imitative of any real Mohammedan building.

58.
Streetcars began running on Warm Springs Avenue in 1891. They made development of the Natatorium a practical venture.

59.
John C. Paulsen's Natatorium was Boise's most exotic building. Its Moorish towers were six stories high. From 1892 until 1933 it was a center of social and recreational activity.

60.
Wooden arches 80 feet in diameter gave the Natatorium interior an impressive spaciousness. The swimming tank is still in use as an open-air pool located behind Adams School.

61.
Selden B. Kingsbury's stone and shingle house at 1225 Warm Springs Avenue was one of the Avenue's showplaces in the late Nineties.

62.
The Bishops' House was built for the Episcopal Bishops of Idaho in the 1880's and enlarged in the 1890's. A major preservation and restoration effort by volunteers has made its Queen Anne elegance available to future generations. The House is now located near the Old Penitentiary.

59

60

61

62

White City Park, next to the Natatorium, was a later development which afforded Boiseans a wide range of amusements through the years. The replacement of streetcars by buses in the late twenties, and the destruction of the "Nat" in 1934 after it had been damaged by a windstorm, marked the end of an era. The city has not had a comparable amusement center linked to public transportation since.

John C. Paulsen did six buildings in Boise between 1891 and 1893, although he himself was only occasionally present in the Boise office he established as a branch of his much larger Helena operation. They show the range of styles eclectic architects of the day were able to provide to their clients, and they also show Paulsen using only slight variations on successful Montana projects completed earlier. In August of 1889, for example, he had completed a moorish revival natatorium outside Helena for railroad magnate Col. C. A. Broadwater. Although its towers were lower and located differently, its interior arrangement and structure were very similar to the Boise Natatorium. No doubt H. B. Eastman and the other promoters of the hot water development called Paulsen to Boise because of this earlier success.

The City Hall and Columbia Threatre projects were both given to Paulsen through the influence of Mayor James A. Pinney. Following closely the style of the Montana Club in Helena which he had designed a year earlier, Paulsen produced for the city a Rhenish Romanesque castle in red brick trimmed in local sandstone. Its tall corner tower was much like the one on the club, and would be repeated later at the normal school in Dillon while Paulsen was State Architect for Montana. After its completion in 1893, Boise's City Hall was the symbol of community pride for a generation. Many mourned its loss when it was torn down in 1953 to make way for a drug store building on the corner of Eighth and Idaho.

The Columbia Theatre, built for theatrical producer Mayor Pinney, was a remarkable eclectic exercise. Its stick and shingled upper facade, with two towers, recalled the medieval north of Europe. Its striped brick lower front, with two arched openings supported on a bulging column, seems Mediterranean, or almost Moorish. Paulsen used the same wooden truss arches he had used in his two natatorium designs. James Pinney himself tore down the Columbia Theater in 1908 when he built the much larger Pinney Theater across the street. Both were on Jefferson between 8th and 9th.

Two houses and an apartment block completed Paulsen's Boise work. He designed a two-towered two-story building on the south side of Idaho east of Sixth for Attorney R. Z. Johnson. The panic of 1893 prevented the further extension of this row as originally intended, but its brick and half-timbered Romanesque picturesqueness still graces the district known as Old Boise. Its front bays, capped with conical roofs, are reminiscent of the lost City Hall. The Queen Anne shingled house at 203 Main, now Graeber's, is

63.
James A. Pinney, a pioneer stationer, was elected Mayor of Boise five times. He commissioned John C. Paulsen to design a City Hall and the Columbia Theatre.

64.
Boise's 1893 City Hall, at the southeast corner of Eighth and Idaho Streets, was a castle in red brick and sandstone.

65.
The Columbia Theatre opened in 1893 with Shakespeare's "As You Like It." The Theater stood in the 800 block on the north side of Jefferson Street across from the later Pinney Theater.

66.
Paulsen's Queen Anne Northrop-Hawley House at 203 Main (now Graeber's) used gambrel gables.

67.
Rhenish Romanesque, like the old City Hall, John C. Paulsen's apartment block designed for R.Z. Johnson had twin towers and a half-timbered second story. It stands at 515 Idaho Street.

64

65

66

67

notable for a wide Richardsonian entry arch, a gambrel roof, and fine beveled plate glass windows.

68.
W.S. Campbell's landmark Idanha Hotel's distinctive towers have graced the corner of Tenth and Main Street since the start of this century. It is a fairy-tale castle in the French Chateau style, considered "modern" in its day.

Although earlier Boise had been built by carpenters and mason contractors without benefit of architects, the Nineties saw a great influx of men with training in the field. As the Statesman explained in July, 1892, "The demand has been steadily increasing for buildings that combine architectural beauty with substantiality. With the demand for better and costlier residence and business structures, naturally (comes) the demand for architects to formulate plans and specifications. For a brief period amateurs were employed to do this work, but the results soon proved unsatisfactory, and a more experienced class of architects soon made Boise their home and found plenty of opportunity to display their skill."

Among those attracted to the capital city's building boom in the Nineties were W. S. Campbell, Chesney & Schroeder, William Houtz, M. Leach, Dixon & Lewis, John E. Tourtellotte, and Charles F. Hummel. Campbell and Tourtellotte formed offices whose successors are still in practice more than 80 years later.

W. S. Campbell

William Stewart Campbell designed a spectacular Grove Street Queen Anne mansion for State Treasurer Frank R. Coffin in 1891 that was perhaps the premiere example of the style Boise has seen. It had a tall round corner tower, lots of gingerbread ornamentation, and one of the best planted and landscaped yards in town. Judging from old photographs, it was the crowning achievement of Grove Street's mansion row — and the last. Warm Springs Avenue and then Harrison Boulevard would gain pre-eminence as fashionable residential locations while Grove Street was gradually rebuilt into a commercial street. (So much so that its last trees could be counted on the fingers of one hand by 1970.)

In 1892, Campbell, a Scotsman, was joined by I. Hodgson of Minneapolis, formerly of Hodgson & Sons, architects, who had done important work in Montana as well as the Middle West. This association was shortlived, and Campbell's best known works in the Nineties were done under his own name. The continuing popularity of the Romanesque revival is shown in the architect's telephone building of 1899. Built on the lot formerly occupied by the Stone Jug on the south side of Main west of Sixth, the building Campbell designed has a facade which is curiously medieval and Richardsonian on the first floor, with three round arches in rusticated stone, and smoothed out and plain on the second. It is part of the National Register Boise Historic District. In 1900, Charles W. Wayland arrived in Boise and went to work as a draftsman in Campbell's office. In 1902 he was made a partner, and when Campbell left for Scotland in 1904, Wayland took over the firm. In his last years in Boise, W. S. Campbell did some of the most important buildings in the city.

68

69

70

71

72

69.
The Romanesque Revival and Boise sandstone were well suited to each other. The 1899 Telephone Building at 609 Main Street shows the massive arches and rusticated stone typical of the style.

70.
Campbell's Federal Building of 1902 demonstrates that architects of the turn of the century had to design in many styles. Having worked in Chateau and Romanesque modes, the architect now designed a courthouse in Classical and Renaissance forms.

71.
The First National Bank of Idaho building which stood at the southwest corner of Eighth and Main Streets, was also Classical. It had an exceptionally fine terra cotta cornice and frieze and was familiar to Boiseans for many years as the location of Link's School of Business.

72.
Granite Hall, at 1205 Warm Springs Avenue, was one of Boise's first Colonial Revival houses. More Georgian than Colonial, this style owes more to 18th Century England than to Colonial America.

73.
Central Fire Station's most interesting features were lost for a time. The bell tower, needed to call volunteer firemen in 1903, was obsolete as soon as it was built. The stone arches became too small for motorized fire trucks.

74.
Restoration of the Station at Sixth and Idaho Streets to its original form was a worthy project, compatable with other restorations in the Boise Historic District, of which it is a part.

73

74

75

75.
This turn-of-the-century photo of a Main Street parade shows the new Falk-Bloch store of 1896 at left and the 1894 Pioneer Block at right. The First National Bank's 1902 building had not yet been built on the Eighth Street corner at lower right. Main Street was now paved, and utility poles lined the sidewalks, filling the space overhead with a maze of wires. Table Rock is conspicuous in the background.

The Idanha Hotel is perhaps his masterpiece, although his 1902 addition to St. Alphonsus hospital was in the same French chateau style. The Idanha, first conceived in 1899, was opened on January 1, 1901. It was the state's grandest hotel, and its turreted picturesqueness echoed, though hardly rivaled, the chateau style hotels built across the continent by the Canadian Pacific company, of which Chateau Frontenac in Quebec was the grandest. If less rambling and picturesque, the Idanha has a grace and elegance not possessed by the more massive Canadian hotels. Campbell was also architect of Boise's federal building at Eighth and Bannock (1902), now known as Borah station, the YMCA building on Tenth between Main and Grove (1901), the Chinese Masonic Hall on Idaho between Seventh and Eighth (1902), the First National Bank building on the southwest corner of Eighth and Main (1902-03), and the Central Fire Station (1903).

The YMCA Building, lost to urban renewal, had a massive three-arched Romanesque revival entry, showing the power of H. H. Richardson's influence nearly two decades after his death. The First National Bank building was an Italian Renaissance revival structure with exceptionally fine classical terra cotta in its ornate cornice. A curious feature of the building was that a local labor dispute in the sandstone quarries led the builders to import stone from Tenino, Washington. Since Boise had become an exporter of its excellent building stone to all parts of the United States in this period, this was like carrying coals to Newcastle.

"Granite Hall," the Georgian revival house of R. M. Davidson, "the Butte, Montana, millionaire" was completed in 1901 by W. S. Campbell at 1205 Warm Springs at a cost of $15,000. It has two distinctions: its early use in Boise of the Colonial revival style, then spreading across the country, and its use of granite. Although a quarry was opened up within a few miles of the city, the materials could not compete with the more plentiful and easily worked sandstone.

Architect Campbell suddenly left Boise at the height of his career, but is known to have worked in Canada later.

Other Architects

Chesney & Schroeder designed only one building still standing in Boise. Beth Israel synagogue at the northwest corner of 11th and State is a Moorish revival structure of wood and sandstone unique for its use of shingles to imitate courses of stone. It has many windows in geometric patterns of amber glass, highlighted by a large Moorish arched window in the south facade. The Falk brothers, who with Moses Alexander were founders of the congregation, commissioned Chesney & Schroeder to do their big new store building at Eighth and Main, also in 1895, but when they decided to build in brick rather than stone, McCaw & Martin of Portland got the job. The last reference to W. R. Chesney comes in

76.
David Falk was a leader of the small but influential Jewish Community in Boise. D. Falk and Brother was a Main Street store from 1868. Falk was president of the congregation when Temple Beth Israel was built in 1895.

77.
Moses Alexander, America's first Jewish governor, became a Boise community leader when he arrived in 1890. He served as Mayor twice before his election to two terms as Governor of Idaho.

78.
Temple Beth Israel at Eleventh and State Streets is a charming example of the Moorish Revival. Shingle patterns imitate courses of stone – a feature more obvious when the building was painted in two tones.

79.
Falk-Bloch & Co. built this big brick "emporium" at Eighth and Main in 1896. A later renovation now covers the ornamented facade.

80.
Moses Alexander's 1897 mansion at Third and State is a fine example of the Queen Anne style. Its ornament, once emphasized by contrasting colors of paint, was later obscured with solid white.

81.
Frank R. Coffin's Pioneer Building of 1894 replaced the old tin shop of 1864. This photo from the 1930s shows that tinware was still made and sold there. It stood at the southeast corner of Eighth and Main Streets.

78

79

80

ALEXANDER HOUSE

81

HARDWARE
STOVES & TIN
MINING SUPPLIES
HARDWARE
PLUMBING DEPT

the Statesman in February, 1896, when he was awarded the contract for a one-story building to be erected on Idaho between Eighth and Ninth, in which the Falk-Bloch company would transact business while their new store at Eighth and Main was being built. There is no mention of Schroeder, who had presumably left Boise, and Chesney soon followed.

Frank R. Coffin tore down the 1864 B. M. Durell building at Eighth and Main in 1894 to erect his three-story brick Pioneer Building. He had a grand celebration in honor of his fellow pioneers of the 1860s, at which he fed them a banquet in the old building. Calling the new one "the most imposing pile in the city," the Statesman said that "the plans, which were drawn by a local architect, are being revised by K. K. Cutter, the Spokane architect." Cutter, who operated Spokane's most prolific and profitable office from 1889 until his retirement in the 1920's, had designed the Idaho building at the Chicago Fair of 1893. He also did two Warm Springs Avenue houses at the end of his career, which will be mentioned later.

Residential Additions

Harrison Boulevard, laid out in the mid-90s, was one of a number of North End developments masterminded by the city's first real estate man. No promoter in Boise history would equal the record of Walter E. Pierce, who came to the city in 1890 in partnership with John M. Haines, later mayor and governor, and L. H. Cox. It was Pierce's custom to have an especially elegant house built for himself in each new addition. As these neighborhoods developed, Pierce sold out and moved to the next where the pattern was repeated. His partners did the same.

Two of these houses are still notable in Idaho history. The 1891 gingerbread "cottage" at 10th and Franklin, designed by John E. Tourtellotte, was one of the most decorative in the city. Embodying the favorite elements of the Queen Anne style, its architectural distinction was given historical significance when William E. Borah, rising young Boise attorney, bought it for his bride, Mamie, daughter of Governor William J. McConnell, in 1895. Since the Borahs spent most of their lives in Washington, D.C. after his election to the U.S. Senate in 1906, their tenure at 10th and Franklin was necessarily brief. The house was moved to the valley west of Garden City in the 1950s when Boise High school expansion threatened it with demolition. Pierce's other "historic" house is the big two-story bungalow at 1905 North 21st Street, which has been the home of Idaho's governors since 1947. Pierce had it built in 1914 from the designs of Wayland & Fennell.

Other Tourtellotte Queen Anne style houses of the Nineties may still be seen in the older parts of the city. So fond of the towered style were Tourtellotte and his clients that there is a local tradition of calling the turrets "Tourtellottes". There were also many smaller cottages in the style without the elegance of turrets, and even

82.
Walter E. Pierce was Boise's leading real estate promoter from 1890 until 1930. He built many of the city's important commercial and residential buildings and was the developer of Harrison Boulevard.

83.
Harrison Boulevard was the first thoroughfare in the city to be built with landscaping. Its park strip, fine homes, and mature shade trees make it a show place.

84.
The Pierce-Borah house, now relocated west of the city, once stood near Boise High School.

85.
The North End is full of fine late Queen Anne houses. This house, at 1403 North 15th, is notable for its tower and corner porch.

86.
A rhythm of dormer windows enlivens the roofline of this house at 2001 North 17th Street. Although Colonial woodwork was coming in (in the Classical Tuscan porch columns) the Queen Anne fancy shingles continued to be popular.

83

84

85

86

without the full decorative treatment all the way around. Boiseans were familiar with a pleasantry about these modest homes that called them "Queen Anne in front, Mary Anne in back."

A mansion which can hardly be described in those terms is the Tourtellotte house at 140 Main, built in 1897-98 for banker Alfred E. Eoff. Called "modern Gothic" at the time, the house is an interesting transitional piece between Queen Anne, with Tudor Gothic porch arches, and Colonial revival details on the interior. James E. Brady of Pocatello bought the house in 1909 when he was elected governor. The L. L. Ormsby house on Idaho, backed up to the Eoff house, was also built in 1897. Although later much enlarged into the apartment block still standing, traces of the original can be seen in the facade, and the superb Ormsby stable still occupies the lot to the east. The Statesman wrote that "Mr. Ormsby has constructed a barn that has not an equal in the state." John E. Tourtellotte was also the architect of these buildings.

Central addition, south of the railroad between Third and Sixth, was a development of the Nineties which also had architectural distinction. Judge George H. Stewart's Queen Anne mansion at Fifth and Myrtle was one of the larger houses built there, and it and a dozen of its neighbors still make up a potential historic district. One other house of the decade merits special mention. It is the square-towered brick mansion of James H. Bush at Eleventh and Franklin, completed in 1892 by J. W. Brown, "architect and builder." Bush, a pioneer freighter and proprietor of the Central Hotel since the Seventies, started to build his mansion shortly after the old hotel at Seventh and Idaho burned to the ground. The Bush house is especially notable for its finely crafted stone window casings set in brick walls and the rich beveled plate and colored glass they surround. Bush mansion is a fine example of adaptive re-use.

Another 1892 building given new life by a change of use is the Grand Army of the Republic Hall on State street, next to St. Michael's Cathedral. William Houtz, its designer-contractor, had previously been "architect and builder" of nearly the entire town of DeLamar, including the mill, tramway, and hotel. The *Owyhee Avalanche* called him a "master mechanic." The G.A.R. Hall is now a photographer's studio and gallery.

South Boise had been platted with new subdivisions by 1890, and the construction of a new steel bridge across the river on Broadway Avenue in 1892 led to increased development. In 1894, the Second Presbyterian church was built at Broadway and Rossi. Later moved to 1020 West Boise Avenue, this wooden Gothic revival building was demolished in 1977. In 1902, the village of South Boise was established, with trustees appointed by the Ada County Commissioners. When street car service was extended across Broadway bridge in 1905, the village became a convenient suburb for those who worked and shopped in the city.

87.
Although modified from its original appearance, the Judge Stewart house at Fifth and Myrtle is a reminder that Central Addition was a fashionable neighborhood.

88.
The Grand Army of the Republic built this hall in 1892. Garrett Photography has adapted the historic structure to a studio and gallery at 714 State Street.

89.
The 1897 Eoff-Brady house at 140 Main Street was built for a banker and later owned by a governor. Its curious mixture of styles reflects the architectural tastes of the turn of the century.

90.
The James H. Bush house at 1020 West Franklin is an elegant 1892 Queen Anne in brick and stone.

91.
This residence at 100 Main Street is a turn-of-the-century Colonial and Queen Anne remodeling of an older farmhouse and has been recently restored.

92.
The State Street Historic District contains a number of fine houses, including this Queen Anne at 210 West State. The bulky tower finial is an unusual feature.

89

91

92

93.
This view, from the top of the new Capitol dome, was made in 1913, looking west. Prominent structures, from left to right, are the Independent Telephone Company, First Baptist Church, First Methodist Church, and First Presbyterian Church. The first three were on Tenth Street, the last on Ninth. Columbia Park is in the foreground – site of the Columbia Theater, demolished in 1908.

94.
Local sandstone was carved into elegant and correct Classical ornament to decorate Tourtellotte & Hummel's State Capitol of 1905-20. Stone on the dome is laid over a steel framework.

Clarence Darrow was so surprised at the architecture and cultural attainments of Boise City in 1906 that he called it "the Athens of the desert." He had come to defend Big Bill Haywood against confessed murderer Harry Orchard's claim that Haywood and the Western Federation of Miners had hired him to blow up former Governor Frank Steunenberg in December, 1905. Darrow found time to add to the city's cultural climate by giving a lecture on the poetry of Walt Whitman at the Columbia Theater.

Development of Idaho's lumber industry, as well as continued expansion of irrigation acreage, contributed to Boise's rapid growth after the turn of the century. From about 6000 people in 1900, the city jumped to over 17,000 in 1910, then leveled off to about 21,000 in 1920. The same rapid growth took place all across southern Idaho in the first ten years of the century, as the Twin Falls, North Side, and Minidoka projects opened up and Boise and Payette river projects brought thousands of new acres under irrigation. Extensive promotion in the midwest and the founding of the new towns of Twin Falls, Rupert, Burley, and Jerome all created an expanding market in which the capital city shared. The decision of the Barber Lumber Company of Wisconsin to construct a sawmill and town for workers on the Boise River a few miles east of the city also was a factor in the new boom. This was a parent company of Boise Cascade.

Downtown had grown impressively in the Nineties. Three-story brick and stone buildings dotted Main and Eighth streets by 1900. These included the Boise City National Bank, Masonic Hall, McCarty Block, I.O.O.F. Hall, City Hall, Lemp Block, and Pioneer Block. Four and six-story buildings would be built between 1901 and 1913, and the new State Capitol's domed central section would be completed in the same period. The street car network had been expanded to serve all of the new residential areas; electric lights and telephone service (started in the mid Eighties) were now used by nearly all businesses and most homes. In fact, since there were two telephone systems, many merchants had to subscribe to both to be available to their customers. Street paving, begun in 1897, was rapidly expanded, and concrete sidewalks extended miles into the suburbs.

The 1901 Idanha Hotel, described earlier, was Boise's first six story building, marking the start of a "skyscraper" era for the city. The Overland Building (1905), the Owyhee Hotel (1909-10), the Idaho Building (1911), the Empire Building (1912), and the Elks Building (1913) all loomed above the rest of downtown. The Idaho building alone of this group was designed outside Boise. Walter E. Pierce, who promoted the project, traveled to Chicago to secure the services of Henry John Schlacks (1868-1938), an architect with a large practice who is best remembered for his metropolitan Chicago churches, including 1921 additions to Holy Name Cathedral.

95.
Construction of the Barber Mill and company town, east of Boise, was one of a number of developments which fed the city's growth in the first decade of the century. The old dam is still there, a new mill operates nearby, and the townsite is now a mobile home subdivision.

96.
The Owyhee Hotel, at Eleventh and Main, opened in 1910 and took its turn as the city's finest hostelry. Its roof garden was the first to take advantage of the foothills view.

97.
The Elks Building and Pinney Theater made an impressive duo at Ninth and Jefferson when this photo was made in the Twenties.

98.
The Idaho Building at Eighth and Bannock, completed in 1911, is Boise's only "Chicago Style" tall building. Henry J. Schlacks of Chicago designed it for Walter E. Pierce.

95

OWYHEE HOTEL
OWYHEE HOTEL
WESTERN AUTO SUPPLY CO.
NO. 150. OWYHEE HOTEL, BOISE, IDAHO

97

98

ALEXANDER'S

Schlacks' Idaho Building well illustrates Louis Sullivan's concept of the skyscraper as a series of functional units, contributing to a total dynamic composition: a basement for mechanical services; a first floor and related second floor for stores and shops; a series of office floors which all look alike "because they are alike," and a top story which has the same function as the capital on a classical column — to gracefully accent and finish the composition. None of Boise's early commercial buildings were tall enough to express Sullivan's ideal, however, of a building that had ". . .the force and power of altitude . . . the glory and pride of exaltation. ."
None achieved his ideal of "every inch a proud and soaring thing," unless it be the Empire building of Nisbet & Paradice.

John E. Tourtellotte & Co.

The firm of John E. Tourtellotte & Co. dominated Boise architecture in the early years of the century. The population tripled between 1900 and 1910, and Tourtellotte's office secured most of the big commissions in Boise and across the state as well. A Connecticut Yankee of Huguenot extraction, Tourtellotte was educated in Webster and Worcester, Massachusetts, where he served apprenticeships with an architect and several building contractors. He worked on construction projects in Chicago, Kansas City, New Mexico, and Colorado before coming to Boise in 1890. After 1894 he no longer did contracting, since his Queen Anne houses had became popular enough that he could make a living as an architect.

In 1900, Tourtellotte was joined by German-born and trained Charles F. Hummel, twelve years his senior. Hummel had also worked as a designer-contractor after coming to Boise in 1895, having earlier spent ten years in Puget Sound cities. The two made a good team, and their long practical experience in construction won the confidence of business men, school boards, church elders, and government officials. They also had a vast repertory of styles at their fingertips, the stock in trade of successful architects in that eclectic period when the romantic associations a building could evoke were as important as its internal arrangements and construction. Frederick C. "Fritz" Hummel, son of C. F. Hummel, who worked in the office when he was still attending Boise High School, and returned after finishing his studies at the University of Pennsylvania, remembered best Tourtellotte's skill in dealing with clients, as well as his kindliness to a young draftsman. (To Fritz at 92, his father's partner was still "Mr. Tourtellotte".)

The Union Block on Idaho Street between Seventh and Eighth was the first joint project of Tourtellotte and Hummel (although their names would not appear together in the firm name until 1912). Of massive sandstone construction, this medieval two-story building is Romanesque in character, even though the principal arches in its facade are segmental rather than round. Moses Alexander and General John Green, former Commandant at Boise Barracks, were

99.
The massive sandstone Union Block in the 700 Block of Idaho Street used Romanesque forms. Part of it has been covered with a modern false-front.

100.
They sang "The Watch on the Rhine" and cheered Teddy Roosevelt when the Boise City Turnverein Building at Sixth and Main was dedicated in 1906. The German-American social and athletic club had been active in Boise since 1870. It now houses a popular restaurant.

101.
The Larsen, Whipple and Tate Buildings were all built on Main Street in 1904. This view shows them from the corner of Eleventh. Demolished 1991.

102.
Moving one block east, the photographer recorded the buildings between Tenth and Eleventh. The brick and stone Gem-Noble block at the corner dominates the scene. A coat of gray paint hides the building's contrasting colors and textures.

99

100

101

102

the developers of the project, which cost $35,000. By the beginning of 1902, the Union Block was nearly all rented out. One historic use, continuing to the present, was a dancing academy.

St. Michael's Episcopal cathedral was another imposing sandstone building used first in 1902. The Episcopalians had secured plans for a "pure-English Gothic" church from New York architect Henry M. Cogdon. Tourtellotte & Co. supervised construction — a project only completed half a century later when the corner tower at Eighth and State streets was finally built. The firm also did the brick and sandstone Gem Block at Tenth and Main in 1902. This was a three-way project for Sigmund Falk, Gibbons & Knight, and John Noble. The Noble Block of 1904 on Main would complete the structure with its round turret at the corner.

Many neighboring buildings also were built within a two year span, giving the west end of Main an architectural distinction it had lacked earlier. Successful real estate promoter W. E. Pierce commissioned Tourtellotte & Co. to do a turreted bank building at Tenth (known as the Men's Wardrobe in 1975 when it was torn down to make way for One Capital Center), and the Larson, Tate, and Whipple blocks were all completed in 1904.

Other significant commissions completed in the first decade of the century were: the Christian Science church on State Street, called "Grecian temple style" at the time, but considerably altered since; the imposing First Methodist church at Tenth and State, (both 1903); and Dr. Boeck's elegant 1904 Romanesque revival office building on Eighth, north of Bannock (demolished 1978). Tourtellotte & Co. also did the Odd Fellows Hall at Ninth and Idaho (1904), and began the Carnegie Library on Jefferson street. Combining Romanesque and Italian renaissance forms, the library was successfully remodeled into law offices in the 1970s.

1905 saw Tourtellotte and Hummel successful in three major competitions for buildings which would assure the firm lasting fame. They won commissions for the State Capitol, with a graceful design which imitated the National Capitol (as did virtually all other capitols in the land at that time) the Administration Building for the University of Idaho at Moscow, with a Tudor Gothic towered building, and a Romanesque St. John's Cathedral for Boise. State Capitol construction was in two phases. The central block with its neo-classical revival portico and tall dome was built between 1905 and 1912. The wings housing Senate and House of Representatives chambers were completed in 1920. Now center of the Capitol Historic District, the Statehouse is notable for its giant interior Corinthian columns of scagliola, a hard polished plaster which imitates marble. Real marble was used on most interior surfaces, and several other varieties of stone augment the Boise sandstone of which the bulk of the structure is made.

103.
Idaho's Statehouse, begun in 1905 and completed in 1920, is one of the better proportioned state capitols in the country. The graceful Corinthian portico is especially pleasing. The rusticated ground floor courses remind some of the logs in a pioneer cabin.

104.
The giant Corinthian columns in the Capitol rotunda are of scagliola – a classic plaster technique which imitates marble. The architectural space they surround is one of the most impressive in Idaho.

105.
An English parish church served as the model for St. Michael's Episcopal Cathedral at Eighth and State Streets. The Gothic theme is enhanced by fine stained glass, including some from the Tiffany studio.

106.
Tourtellotte & Hummel's Carnegie Library at 815 Washington Street is today a good example of the adaptive re-use of historic Boise buildings – a trend which came into its own in the 1970s.

103

104

105

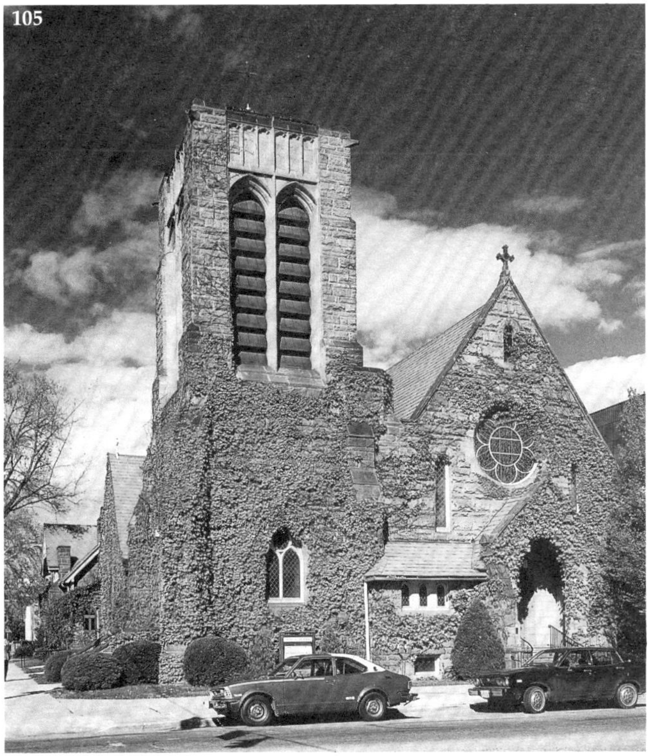

106

Although the cornerstone for St. John's Cathedral was laid in 1906, it was many years before the imposing Romanesque revival building was completed. Traditional in form, and based in part on the German Cathedral of Mainz, with details borrowed from English examples as well, St. John's is of rusticated Boise sandstone with three round-arched doorways at its east end topped by a giant wheel window. Its stained glass and richly polychromed interior make it one of the city's most impressive.

In 1894 the pioneers had gathered to say farewell to the 1864 B. M. Durell-Frank Coffin building at Eighth and Main. Ten years later they convened again for a last nostalgic reunion just before the 1864 Overland hotel on the opposite corner was torn down. Tourtellotte & Co. designed the new Overland building as a four-story Second Renaissance Revival palazzo with a course of round-arched windows on the top floor under a classical terra cotta cornice decorated with rows of grinning lion heads. Later enlarged to six stories, the building was renamed Eastman building in 1927 to honor H. B. and Ben Eastman, proprietors of the old hotel and builders of the new block. The ornate carved sandstone doorway on Eighth Street bears their name and the dates 1864-1905, in memory of the earlier landmark.

After 1905 this historic principal intersection of the downtown boasted at its four corners the Overland Building, the Pioneer Building (1894), the Falk-Bloch Building (1896), and the First National Bank Building (1902). Boise definitely had a "big city" look, which was a matter of considerable local pride, especially after Tourtellotte & Hummel's Owyhee Hotel (1909-10) was followed by Schlacks' Idaho Building, Nisbet & Paradice's Empire Building, and their own Elk's Building in 1913. Not until the Hotel Boise was completed in 1930 would the skyline receive another major addition, even though dozens of smaller brick structures filled most of the vacant lots downtown in the years between.

By a painful reverse process, the automobile, which began to dominate the life style of Americans in the same period, would demand that dozens of these same buildings be razed for parking lots — a perforating of the urban fabric which would eventually call into being massive urban renewal projects to save the cities. Unfortunately for the sense of place and individual identity cherished by most Americans, the renewal process would go on demolishing familiar landmarks to make way for future redevelopment until most cities had the "bombed-out" look familiar to Boiseans in the 1970s.

107.
The massive facade of St. John's Roman Catholic Cathedral at Eighth and Hays is Romanesque in style. Major restoration of the stained glass and interior decoration has recently been completed.

108.
The Eastman Building at Eighth and Main was an Italian Renaissance Revival commercial block, begun in 1905. Two additional stories were added in 1910 and the original cornice was moved upward.

109.
The Fraternal Order of Eagles occupied this three-story brick building at Sixth and Idaho Streets in 1912. The cornice is representative of the fine craftsmanship in brick current at the time.

110.
Boise High School at 1010 Washington Street was erected in several stages. It has an especially pure Greek portico in the Ionic Order and is a good example of the Neo-Classic style.

107
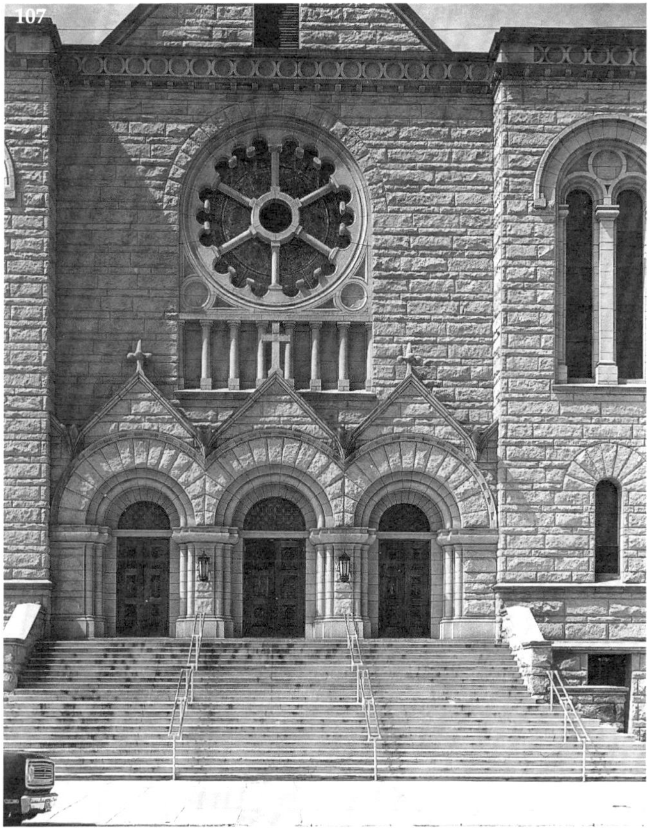

108

109

110

Wayland & Fennell

Wayland & Fennell, successors to Campbell & Wayland after 1904, had an architectural practice in Idaho rivalling that of Tourtellotte & Hummel. Charles W. Wayland, a Bostonian, got his early training in Duluth, Minnesota. He came to Boise in 1900 and, after only two years as a draftsman for William S. Campbell, was made a partner in Campbell & Wayland. James M. Fennell was a Californian. After completing one of the earliest degree courses in architecture, he practiced in Butte, Montana from 1897 until 1902, when he came to Boise and went to work with Campbell. Familiar Boise buildings by Wayland & Fennell are the 1910 Idaho Statesman building at Sixth and Main, (a fine Georgian Revival two-story brick structure), and the Tiner and McCarty buildings. Wayland & Fennell also prepared plans for a handsome neo-classical joint county-city building in the spring of 1908, but a bond election that fall failed. They did get to do a building of similar character in 1914 to represent Idaho at San Francisco's Panama-Pacific Exposition.

Nisbet & Paradice

The Empire Building is the best known work of Nisbet & Paradice, also known in Boise for their many residential designs. A native of Pittsburgh, Benjamin Morgan Nisbet graduated in architecture from the University of Pennsylvania in 1898. He came to Boise in 1903, and worked for Tourtellotte & Co. until 1909, when he formed his own firm in partnership with Frank H. Paradice. While with Tourtellotte, Nisbet had worked on the Capitol, St. Johns, and the Overland Building. Paradice also was well educated and had served his apprenticeship before coming to town. He had graduated from the Chicago Art Institute and Armour Institute of Technology before working in Denver and Portland. In 1914, Nisbet moved his office to Twin Falls and Paradice went to Pocatello. The Yates building, formerly at 9th and Main, was also a Nisbet & Paradice design. It housed a bank and Moses Alexander's store until the former governor built his new building across the street in 1924.

111.
Wayland & Fennell's 1910 Idaho Statesman building at 6th & Main is in another Classical style, popular in its day: the Georgian Revival. This was the Statesman's third home since 1864. It has had two others since.

112.
The McCarty building at Ninth and Idaho was also a product of the Wayland & Fennell partnership. Its zig-zag cornice motif is rare in Boise.

113.
Nisbet & Paradice's most important Boise project was the Empire Building, now known as the Idaho First National Bank Building at Tenth and Idaho Streets. Although it employs classical details in an unusual way, the general effect suggests Adler & Sullivan's famous Wainwright Building in St. Louis.

114.
The substantial and well-proportioned Yates Building, which stood at Ninth and Main, housed the Boise State Bank and Alexander's store before World War I. Note that it followed an old tradition of Idaho banks – a corner entrance.

111

112

113

114

115

116

117

115.
The Belgravia at Fifth and Main, originally the Dubois Flats of 1904, was converted to shops and offices in the 1970s.

116.
Industrial structures were richly ornamented in the tradition of commercial buildings, as in Idaho Power Company's 1910 substation at 601 South 17th Street.

117.
Hyde Park at 13th and Eastman was a neighborhood shopping center in the North End – perhaps the first satellite area to Boise's downtown.

118.
Mutual Creamery building in the Eighth Street Historic District is a fine example of early 20th Century brick work. Although employing some traditional masonry forms, it clearly looks ahead to the crispness of modern architectural functionalism.

119.
The Eighth Street wholesale district was built south of the railroad tracks in the decade after 1902. Now part of a National Register Historic District, these buildings are being redeveloped for shops, restaurants, and other commercial uses.

120.
New landscaping, a median strip, paved walks, and restoration of original street lights, augments renovation of the historic Eighth Street warehouse buildings.

118

119

120

121.
Boating in a man-made lake was one of the attractions at Pierce Park in the golden age of electric street railways. The Interurban Company built it to give patrons a destination.

122

122.
The Daly house at 1015 West Hays Street is a classic Colonial Revival by the architects of the State Capitol, Tourtellotte & Hummel. As in the Capitol, the portico is Corinthian.

In the first twenty years of the new century, Boise's residential areas spread rapidly outward from the old city center. The street car lines sometimes followed, but usually preceded, development of new neighborhoods. This inexpensive and reliable public transportation was an important factor in making the suburbs popular, especially after the Interurban route westward to Middleton and Caldwell was completed in 1907. Nampa had service by 1910 and the "loop" was completed in 1912. Real estate speculators, following the pattern of railway land companies earlier, attempted to start new towns along the electric lines. Dr. H. P. Ustick's plat of a townsite five miles west of Boise is an example, and several brick buildings, including a bank and general store, remain of this 1908 promotion, still called Ustick.

Between 1912 and 1930, no new tall buildings were erected downtown. The Boise Board of Trade, later the Chamber of Commerce, shifted its promotional emphasis from the skyline to homes. "Boise is Essentially a City of Homes" proclaimed a 1915 headline in the Idaho Statesman's annual summary of the previous year's progress. This newspaper feature, symptomatic of the dream of every small American town to become a big city, was repeated for many years. Special supplements were printed, with glowing descriptions of Boise's advantages of climate, business opportunity, and cultural achievements. It was an age of "boosterism", and Boards of Trade and local newspapers did not spare the adjectives.

There is no doubt, however, that a laudable idealism accompanied these desires for economic growth. Boise faced the fact for the first time that progress had a price. In 1904, the Chamber of Commerce asked the City Council to take action to save the trees which gave Boise its traditional name. Noting "the wanton destruction of shade trees by the utility companies," and "the unsightly array of telephone, telegraph, and electric light wires which now disfigure the streets of Boise", the Idaho Statesman also urged preservation of "Boise the Beautiful."

This name, which the city adopted in promotional booklets done from 1895 onward, reflected Boise's awareness of a national City Beautiful movement, given great impetus by the Chicago Fair of 1893. Architects, artists, and landscape designers had collaborated there to create a beautiful and coordinated environment on a grand and dramatic scale. Public buildings in classical style, broad avenues, bridges, and parks became part of a national dream to counteract the ugliness that rapid growth had created across the land.

123.
Interurban streetcars like this one brought Caldwell, Nampa, Middleton and other valley residents to the Capital City.

124.
A bank, general store, and other businesses marked the center of Dr. H.P. Ustick's new town on the Interurban, shown here as they look today.

125.
This old post card view shows White City Park's "scenic railway," with the Natatorium towers in the background.

126.
Moses Alexander built his "big white store" in 1924 after serving two terms as governor. Its white terra cotta surface shows no sign of weathering.

127.
In 1927 the First National Bank of Idaho had Portland architect A.E. Doyle design a new banking room next door to the Empire Building on Idaho Street. Young Pietro Belluschi came to town representing Doyle.

124

125

126

The City Beautiful

The City's first large parks were begun in the period. Thomas Jefferson Davis, one of the 1863 founders, donated part of his original ranch along Boise river to the city to be developed into Julia Davis Park in honor of his wife. Walter E. Pierce created Pierce Park, west of the city on the valley road, as part of the Interurban railway project of 1907. It gave people a destination for family outings where they could picnic, dance in the pavilion, or boat on an artificial lake created for the purpose. Plantation golf course was developed on this property after the Interurban stopped running in 1928. Golf had been played early in the century on a dry course in the foothills with raked sand "greens" instead of grass. Curtis Park near Caldwell was another Interurban project at the other end of the line, and Boise families often took summer picnic hampers there and made a day of it.

White City park, named for Chicago's "Great White City" of 1893, was developed on the grounds of the Natatorium. It had "a scenic railway, a joy wheel, a fun factory, pavilion and skating rink, a picture show building, a band stand that will seat sixty musicians, a miniature railway, a lake for boating in the summer and skating in the winter, an ostrich farm, and other attractions."

The most dramatic development of the City Beautiful concept came in 1925, when the Union Pacific built its new mainline depot on the bench south of downtown. Architects Carrere & Hastings of New York conceived of a grand Capitol Boulevard sweeping from the Statehouse to their Mission style depot. Broad and park-like, this landscaped thoroughfare was never fully carried out as planned, although the graceful memorial bridge over the river was worthy of the original concept. Platt Gardens on the hillside below the depot (a National Register site in its own right) also survives as part of the beauty envisioned by the planners.

Commercial development along the boulevard, with its aggressive signing of all sizes, shapes, and colors, was never controlled by zoning or sign ordinances, and aesthetic review committees and other quasi-governmental bodies appointed from time to time proved largely unable to prevent visual pollution along what could have been a magnificent approach to the city and its graceful capitol dome. The encroachment of large buildings without adequate offset from the boulevard would later mar the effect originally intended still further.

Residential styles of the new century shifted from the popular Queen Anne of the Nineties to Georgian and Colonial Revival first. Characterized by the same classical details made popular by the Chicago Fair, and shining white in color, the new houses were often fronted by graceful temple-like porticos in Tuscan, Ionic, or Corinthian orders. Tourtellotte and Hummel produced three of the best in the style. The 1903 Timothy Regan house at 110 Main is an elegant Corinthian structure with a graceful two story protico which

128.
In 1925 Carrere & Hastings Union Pacific station on the bench was completed in time for the first Mainline train celebration. A new Capitol Boulevard connected it with downtown.

129.
Timothy Regan's Colonial Revival house at 110 Main Street resembles the Daly-Archer house, but has lost its side porches.

130.
Judge Frank Dietrich's Colonial house at 201 West Jefferson has been beautifully maintained.

131.
The L.D.S. Tabernacle was built in 1924 in the popular Colonial style with a Tuscan portico. Demolished in 1992.

128

129

130

131

contrasts with a sandstone main block. Side porches have been removed, but an idea of their appearance can be gained from viewing the 1977-78 restoration of the Daly-Archer house at 1015 West Hays Street, built in 1912.

The L. H. Cox house at 1308 Warm Springs, built for one of the partners of W. E. Pierce & Co., is a wooden classical revival in the Ionic order, although its capitals have unfortunately been lost and need restoration. The Judge Frank Dietrich house at 201 West Jefferson is another especially fine example of the big symmetrical "Colonial" houses of the period. Although little like anything built in colonial America, these revival buildings do possess features reminiscent of some 18th century English houses, especially their classical pediments, pilasters, columns, and Palladian windows. (Dozens of these three-part windows, with a round-arched central one dominant, can be seen in houses in the North End).

133.
A symmetrical bungalow with open trellises flanking the front porch.

134.
This bungalow at 910 North 17th combines a Boise sandstone porch with the half-timbered look.

135.
Multiple "figure four" brackets give a light "stick" character to this bungalow at 1707 Resseguie.

136.
Tile roofs and stucco walls were popular with many Basque families, recalling the provincial farmhouses of the old country. Domingo Aldecoa remodeled this house at 212 East Idaho Street from an earlier bungalow in 1928.

The Bungalow City

"While the bungalow prevails as the chief style, the mission and colonial have their share of admirers," wrote the *Statesman* in its survey of 1908 building progress. By 1912, the *Sunday Capital News* could say that "Boise is becoming known as the bungalow city . . ." and claim that in proportion to population, Boise had even more bungalows than Los Angeles.

Although the name is derived from Bengal in India and a kind of native house adapted by the British colonial army for use in hot climates, the California bungalow owed its form to earlier Spanish colonial houses there, to Japanese, and even New England influences. The mild California climate and the native redwood lumber were also factors in its development. Its rapid spread to Idaho and the rest of the country was assisted by economic factors as much as by the novelty of its style. The cost of building increased by nearly 40% from 1900 to 1907, and the bungalow was cheaper to build than any other kind of house. Just as "cottage" once meant a modest house which working people could afford, "bungalow," too, became synonymous with middle-class housing.

Many kinds of bungalows were built in Boise, but two forms were most numerous: a one-story house with low-pitched gable facing the street, and a two-story house turned the other way with a dormer for more bedroom space upstairs. These dormers were either gabled or shed-roofed. All kinds of bungalows had other features in common. Their roof joists were exposed, and braced with simple square sticks set at a 45 degree angle. Barge boards were often accented at their ends by cut out notches which made them look even lighter. Porches across the fronts of most bungalows were set under the main roof, with square boxed supports sometimes tapering inward at the top. The entire effect was one of lightness and straightforward structural expression, often of the traditional

133

134

135

136

American "stick" style, in which the frame is exaggerated. Although typically of wood with clapboard siding, Boise bungalows also used sandstone or brick lower walls and stucco upper walls, occasionally achieving a "half-timbered" look typical of another popular revival style, the "Tudor" or English cottage.

Most bungalows were built from readily available stock plans, but a few more elegant ones were designed by architects. J. Flood Walker, a Californian who worked in Boise for less than two years before moving on to Texas, designed Governor John T. Morrison's bungalow at 211 West State Street in 1905. Unique among Boise bungalows, Walker's design has been called a "chalet", and, indeed, this was one of the many influences that contributed to the work of the greatest creators in the bungalow mode: Greene & Greene of Pasadena, California. Charles Sumner Greene and his brother Henry Mather Greene designed their first bungalow, based primarily upon Spanish colonial traditions, in 1903, and by 1908 had perfected the style in their magnificent David B. Gambel house at Pasadena, a synthesis of Japanese, American stick, and early California traditions.

If Californian Walker's design owes little to the Greenes, it should be remembered that "the California bungalow" had already attracted national attention by 1905, before their work had. *The Ladies Home Journal* published an article called "The Comfortable Bungalow in California" in January, 1904, and Gustave Stickley's *Craftsman Magazine* had also begun to lean toward the new form as most suited to its own ideal of a house which could shape character and promote domestic tranquility through hand-crafted surroundings.

The Fred Coleman bungalow at 1423 West Franklin, built in 1910 from the plans of Nisbet & Paradice, is perhaps the city's handsomest bungalow. It is certainly one of the most substantial, and of all those built at the time, the most indebted to the influence of Greene & Greene. Built of clinker brick and roofed in tile, it nevertheless manages the open and light look of a more modest bungalow.This effect is enhanced by the slender delicacy of exposed rafter ends and porch rails, and by typical stick brackets. It further expresses the bungalow and Craftsman ideals of continuous space which connects outdoor areas with indoor ones, often centered in a fireplace.

Frank Lloyd Wright, who had similar ideas about space, and who published plans for a $5000 house in the April, 1907, *Ladies Home Journal,* apparently had little influence in Boise. Only the 1913 Charles P. McCarthy house at 1415 Fort Street resembles the Prairie Style very much, although the magazine was read by a large number of Boiseans. The old California ties, going back to 1863, were much stronger than the attraction of a style from the midwest, and many Boiseans traveled regularly to the south for business and winter vacations. (Although J. Flood Walker stayed too short a time to have

137.
Governor John Morrison lived in this "Chalet Style" bungalow at 211 State Street.

138.
Fred Coleman's bungalow at 1423 West Franklin is a substantial brick structure designed by Nisbet & Paradice.

139.
The Charles McCarthy house at 1415 Fort Street has the character of Frank Lloyd Wright's Prairie Style.

140.
The Ison house at 815 Warm Springs Avenue has the wide overhanging eaves and second story corner windows of the Prairie Style.

137

1

139

140

much influence, it should be remembered that James M. Fennell, another Californian, was active in the city for many years as a partner in the leading firm of Wayland & Fennell.)

Mission Style

141

Most obviously Californian in derivation was the Mission style. The white stucco and red tile roofs of this romantic and greatly modified offspring of the early Franciscan missions was popular in Boise from after the turn of the century continuing into the Thirties. The primitive adobe architecture of early California was not well adapted to twentieth century domestic use, and what developed was yet another cloak for older forms. Except for the stucco and tile, many Boise examples have the same shapes as bungalows and colonials. Two striking examples from the Tourtellotte & Hummel office, both done in 1911, are worth noting to show the variation possible within what was called Mission. The Will Regan house at 1009 Warm Springs Avenue extends two one-story tile-roofed pavilions toward the street to create an entry court between. Attic dormers on each advancing wing are similar to a third in the center. Wide eaves give a Prairie Style character to the house, but the interior is pure Craftsman. The architect succeeded in creating a unified effect from a number of stylistic influences.

The G. W. Bond house, 1505 Harrison Boulevard, is a two-story box-shaped house with certain similar devices adding up to a quite different total effect. The tile roof is identical in pitch and texture to the Regan house, with three roof elements much like the Regan dormers. The two flanking units are actually projecting oriel windows supported on brackets, however, although the pavilion effect is still there. A balcony is centered below a pair of windows just below the dormer. Massive columns of primitive character support the front of the house over a wide and deep porch.

There were many commercial buildings in this early Mission style as well, but none has survived. The Boise Automobile Company of 1908, by J. E. Tourtellotte & Co., was a striking baroque example. The Union Pacific depot of 1925 by Carrere & Hastings of New York, began a fresh revival of Mission architecture in Boise, but it is obvious that the style was well-established nationally if an Omaha based railroad could hire New York architects to do a California style building in Idaho. The Southern Pacific and Santa Fe railroads had earlier built many Mission style depots in the southwest, so there was ample precedent for the choice. The Boise depot is one of the city's cherished landmarks, and its slender white clock-and bell-tower is prominent on the southern skyline from downtown, especially when viewed from Capitol Boulevard.

The Women's Columbian Club built a handsome clubhouse in Mission style in 1925 at 9th and Washington. This Wayland & Fennell building was demolished in the Seventies. C. C. Anderson's big new department store, which opened in 1927, also had the

141.
C.C. Anderson's Golden Rule store on Idaho Street, which opened in 1927, was in the tile-roofed Mission Style. Later remodeled as the Bon Marche, the present version no longer shows any Mission character.

142.
The 1911 Will Regan house on Warm Springs Avenue combines California bungalow and Mission features. Tourtellotte & Hummel were the architects.

143.
The G.W. Bond house on Harrison Boulevard is a two-story version of what Boiseans called the California style. The stucco and tile are Mission materials.

144.
Union Pacific's 1925 depot is the city's outstanding example of the Mission Style. Its conspicuous site makes it a highly visible local landmark.

145.
This house at 1608 North 21st is typical of smaller Mission-influenced dwellings built in the 1930s which also have Art Deco features.

144

145

146

familiar Mission round-arched openings and tile roofs fronting Idaho Street. Now the Bon Marche, the Anderson store was later remodeled to remove all traces of its original style.

Concrete and stucco were popular materials of the Mission revival. They were also used in the building of one of Boise's most exotic buildings of the Twenties, Frederick C. Hummel's Egyptian Theater.

When Idaho's grandest movie palace opened in April 1927, with John Barrymore as "Don Juan," first nighters were dazzled by the brilliance of Egyptian art recreated in plaster, gold leaf and color by the German-born architect and a crew of German artisans from Salt Lake City. Inspired by visits to Egyptian-style movie houses in Hollywood and Ogden, and doing his research in the Boise Public Library, Fritz Hummel produced one of the most popular buildings the city has ever had. Thousands of present day Boiseans have shown their support for its preservation by attending benefit performances on the only active theater organ in the state and revivals of silent film classics. A highlight was the 50th anniversary revival of "Don Juan" before a capacity house with the 91-year-old architect present and Gaylord Carter at the console of the Robert Morton "theater orchestra." The fully restored theater now seems sure to grace downtown Boise for many years to come.

Spokane architect Kirtland K. Cutter, mentioned earlier, did his only Boise residences in the Twenties. His 1922 Leo J. Falk house at 1320 Warm Springs Avenue is a Mission-Mediterranean adaptation featuring the use of stucco walls which integrate the garden spaces into the total complex. In 1925, Cutter designed one of the largest houses on the Avenue at 929 Warm Springs for department store magnate C. C. Anderson. English half-timbered in style, the house is picturesquely Tudor on a grand scale. There are many other good examples of the Tudor style, some built as late as 1940. Two early remodelings of Queen Anne houses also produced half-timbered houses of distinction: Tourtellotte & Hummel turned Edgar Wilson's 1902 castle at 103 Warm Springs Avenue into restrained and dignified Tudor, and the Queen Anne at 204 West State Street into the same character.

146.
The Temple of Amon at Karnak inspired the great proscenium columns in the 1927 Egyptian Theater.

147.
Kirtland K. Cutter, famous Spokane architect, designed the 1922 Mission Style Leo J. Falk house at 1320 Warm Springs Avenue.

148.
Fritz Hummel's Egyptian Theater is one of the best examples in America of the 1920s Egyptian Revival style inspired by the discovery of King Tut's tomb.

149.
The Wilson-Mott house at 103 Warm Springs Avenue was remodeled into this Engligh half-timbered cottage after starting out as a Queen Anne castle.

150.
K.K. Cutter's other Boise house was designed for department store magnate C.C. Anderson in 1925. It is a large and impressive example of English half-timbered country house.

Art Deco

The dominant architectural style of the 1930s and 1940s, and the last to be discussed in this brief survey of Boise's buildings, was called "modernistic" at first. Historians see its origins in the Paris Exposition des Arts Decoratifs of 1925, and have called it "Moderne" for that reason, but the term Art Deco seems to be the one that will prevail. Although rejecting the forms and decorative elements of all earlier styles, in common with other 20th Century modern movements in architecture, the Art Deco style was different from most in its frank love of decoration. This ranged from stylized plants and flowers to geometric zig-zags which recall Navaho blankets.

149

One phase of Art Deco emphasized streamlining, transferring to buildings shapes developed for aerodynamic reasons on trains and automobiles. The emphasis in streamlined Art Deco was on the horizontal, with windows pushed to the extreme corners of buildings, often with horizontal muntins.

Porthole windows, semicircular cantilevered porch roofs above semicircular porches and steps, glass brick insets, metal railings, usually made up of parallel horizontal bars — these are all familiar hallmarks of Art Deco. White stucco was the favorite color for Art Deco buildings, but black glass and chrome were popular for trim and interior features like fireplaces.

The Chicago World's Fair of 1933 had great influence in spreading the exotic shapes of an architecture of the future to every corner of America, and Art Deco forms appeared everywhere, inside homes as well as out. Ash trays, radios, refrigerators, and lamps all became streamlined, or covered with zig-zags or stylized plant forms.

Three years before the Chicago fair opened, Boise saw the construction of one of the Pacific Northwest's landmark buildings in Art Deco. Hotel Boise, the work of Frank Hummel, was designed in 1929. Its strong vertical piers ending in projecting finials give it a thrust reminiscent of Gothic, although its panels of decoration, moulded in concrete, are more like the Paris of the 1925 exhibition than the Paris of Notre Dame Cathedral. Alone of Boise's large commercial buildings done before 1938, the hotel is smooth concrete rather than brick. Its penthouse repeats the vertical mood. Giant signs added later gave it an element of pop art which robbed it of its intended character. Happily, in the 1978 renovation of the hotel, the obtrusive, though by now landmark, signs have been removed. A taller penthouse adds grace to the building and is closer to Frank Hummel's first sketches than what was built in 1930.

The Idaho Power Company's building at 1220 West Idaho Street is a good example of zig-zag Art Deco, and its forms repeat the American Indian symbol for lightning — a device also exploited in the "Reddy Kilowatt" character, long used to symbolize electrical companies. Boise High School Gymnasium, North Junior High School, Ada County Courthouse, and a number of residences also illustrate the various forms that Art Deco took in the city. The style continued to be popular after World War II, but is only now sufficiently removed from us in time for an assessment to be made. Like Queen Anne and earlier styles it has passed through a period when it was regarded with contempt, and considered ugly by most observers, into an era of appreciation for its distinctive qualities.

Boise's architectural history is, of course, still unfolding, but the decision to end this brief account before World War II is perhaps justified by the title "Historic Boise," and by the difficulty of analyzing the complex developments of the past forty years within the space available.

151.
Hotel Boise's handsome stylized decorative panels in cast concrete derive directly from the 1925 Paris Exposition des Arts Decoratifs, where nothing was exhibited unless it was "of strictly modern tendency." This "moderne" style was one aspect of what is now usually called Art Deco.

152.
Recently renovated, Hotel Boise now features a new penthouse tower which exploits fine views of the Boise hills, the Capitol, and the rest of the city. Completed originally in 1930, the hotel was a pioneer Art Deco building in the Pacific Northwest.

153.
Idaho Power Company's Idaho Street headquarters is an example of "zig-zag" moderne.

154.
Some Boise Art Deco houses showed all of the characteristic of the style in a small space. This house at 2312 Pleasanton is a good example.

155.
A clean and classic Art Deco house which shows strongly the influence of the International Style is this house at 1115 North 23rd.

152

153

154

155

Historic Preservation

The historic preservation movement in America achieved official significance in 1932 with the creation of the National Register of Historic Places; it was greatly extended with the Historic Preservation Act of 1966, and it has received powerful economic encouragement from the Tax Reform Acts of 1976 and 1978.

A renewed appreciation of the nation's architectural heritage has led to the creation of state and local programs to retain, restore, and recycle buildings with historic and architectural significance. The national energy problem has made preservation a priority, above and beyond the historic or cultural concerns felt earlier. The creation of the Boise Historic Preservation Commission and the publication of this book reflect a national pattern of awareness that our architecture is a resource to be treated with new respect and appreciation. If it contributes to that awareness it will have fulfilled its purpose.

Acknowledgements

I am grateful to a number of people who gave assistance and advice during the preparation of this book. I especially appreciate the insights into Boise's architectural history derived from conversations with the late Frederick C. Hummel, F.A.I.A. Not many architects live long enough to see their buildings listed in The National Register of Historic Places. Not many writers on architecture have access to the counsel and memories of a remarkable informant like Fritz Hummel.

Charles F. Hummel and Glen E. Cline were generous with information and with access to the records of the pioneer architectural firms they represent. Fellow workers at the Idaho State Historical Society whose help is warmly appreciated are Bill Dougall, Don Hibbard, Larry Jones, and Jim Davis. I am especially grateful to Merle Wells for his patient efforts to make me both sceptical and judicious, and for his advice on the main thrusts of Boise's political and economic development.

Members of the Boise Historic Preservation Commission read the manuscript and made suggestions, many of which are incorporated into the final version. Bob Aldridge skillfully edited the punctuation. Research upon which this work is based has occupied the author for ten years. The Idaho Statesman from 1864 onward is the principal source used, but other historic materials, such as city directories, fire maps, and the large photographic collection of the Idaho Historical Society have also been indispensable.

Although it was decided to dispense with footnotes in the interest of readability, citations for the quotations used and for all matters of fact are available at the Idaho Historical Society. The interpretations and conclusions are the author's own.

Arthur A. Hart
Boise, Idaho
1979

INDEX

Photograph Numbers in bold face

Architect or Designer

Buildings

Photography Credits

John Tinker: 1, 13-15, 17, 19-20, 29, 34-36, 39, 51-53, 55, 62, 67-70, 74, 78, 80, 83-92, 94, 98, 100-102, 104, 105, 107, 109-112, 114-120, 122, 124, 126, 127, 129-137, 139, 142-145, 147-149, 152-155.

Idaho State Historical Society: 4-8, 10-12, 16, 18, 21-33, 37, 38, 42-50, 54, 56-61, 63-66, 71-73, 75-77, 79, 81, 82, 93, 95-97, 99, 103, 106, 108, 111, 113, 121, 123, 125, 128, 138, 140, 146, 150.

Duane W. Garrett: 3, 41, 88, 151.
Ada County Recorder: 9, 40.
City of Boise: 2.